UNDERGRADATE TEXTS IN COMPUTER SCIENCE

Editors
David Gries
Fred B. Schneider

Springer Science+Business Media, LLC

UNDERGRADUATE TEXTS IN COMPUTER SCIENCE

Beidler, Data Structures and Algorithms

Kozen, Automata and Computability

Merritt and Stix, Migrating from Pascal to C++

Zeigler, Objects and Systems

Bernard P. Zeigler

Objects and Systems

Principled Design with Implementations in C++ and Java

With 57 Illustrations

 Springer

Bernard P. Zeigler
Department of Electrical
    and Computer Engineering
University of Arizona
Tucson, AZ 85721
USA

Library of Congress Cataloging-in-Publication Data
Zeigler, Bernard P., 1940–
        Objects and systems: principled design with implementations in C++ and Java /
by Bernard P. Zeigler.
                p.   cm. – (Undergraduate texts in computer science)
        Includes bibliographical references and index.
        ISBN 978-1-4612-7335-6   ISBN 978-1-4612-1912-5 (eBook)
        DOI 10.1007/978-1-4612-1912-5
        1. C++ (Computer program language).   2. Java (Computer programming language).
        3. Object-oriented programming (Computer science).   I. Series.
        QA76.73.C153Z45   1996
        005.13'3–dc20   96-18350

Production managed by Frank Ganz; manufacturing supervised by Joe Quatela.
Camera-ready copy prepared from the author's Word files.

9 8 7 6 5 4 3 2 1

ISBN 978-1-4612-7335-6

Preface

Where This Book Fits in; How It Came to Be

Books on C++ and lately, Java, occupy a full shelf at the bookstore and more than adequately cover the mechanical aspects of programming in C++. Books such as Booch's (1991) occupy the high plane of object-oriented design and analysis. Only a few, such as Budd's (1991), attempt to bridge the gap between coding and design, as we do here. Some features in the middle ground that make this book unique are:

- its emphasis on formulating primitives from which all other desired functionality can be built; e.g., we develop primitives for lists and later devote a chapter to an original set of primitives for the containers hierarchy;
- its integral use of semiformal behavior specification language based on straightforward *state-transition* concepts.
- the differentiation between behavior and implementation with many examples.
- its demonstration of a reusable heterogeneous container class library with full specification of each class and implementation in C++ and Java.
- the elegance and power of the ensemble methods working on top of well-known properties (polymorphism, inheritance) — illustrated in nontrivial examples.
- the payoff of the state-transition behavior specification in terms of testing methodology.

An Interview with the Author

Perhaps the easiest way to explain the place and contribution of the approach developed here is to retrace the history of its development. Dropping the third person, I'll do this with an interview with myself.

Q: What motivated you to do this project?

A: When I first started to teach software engineering in 1985, there were no textbooks that could provide concrete guidance as to how to practice the discipline they preached.

The most unifying and rigorous framework came from Wymore's (1967) system engineering concepts, which did not, however, apply to software directly. Fairley's (1985) book became my standard since it provided comprehensive coverage along with some discussion of formal methods that could be used to give meat to a course. Unfortunately, when one tried to follow the paradigm: specification→implementation →verification, it's help quickly evaporated. The situation improved somewhat a few years later as the books by Liskov (1986) and Lamb (1988) appeared. They offered more examples of algebraic and trace specifications. Unfortunately, having derived from academic research, both couched their approaches in mathematical logic that undergraduates could not be expected to understand, let alone use.

Q: How did object orientation enter?

A: The teaching situation improved significantly with the emergence of object-oriented languages in usable form. With such concrete tools, the concepts of information hiding, data abstraction, and so on could be given tangible form.

Q: Why didn't this solve the problem?

A: There was still a disconnect between these widely distributed and commercial languages, such as SMALLTALK, CLOS (Stefik and Bobrow, 1986), and C++ (Stroustrup, 1989); which were developed by the programming community, and their counterpart concepts, being researched by the logic-based researchers.

Q: When did you seriously start to tackle this problem?

A: I first tried to fill this gap during a sabbatical year, 1991, spent with my former student Norman Foo, a logic-based artificial intelligence researcher in Sydney. I felt that the trouble with the logic-based approach was that it obscured the underlying concepts that were evident from early automata and systems theory. Norman's earlier work with me on systems theory made him sympathetic to my approach, although he still believed that logic was the true answer (Foo, 1987). Our unpublished paper (Zeigler and Foo) showed how Nerode's concepts from automata theory (Arbib, 1969) provide a consistent foundation that explains some of the mysteries and anomalies of formal specification. As of this writing, he paper still languishes in review, presumably because no referees can be found to confirm or deny its conclusions.)

Q: What mysteries and anomalies are you talking about?

A: The expressive power of algebraic specification was a puzzle. Could it go beyond the standard textbook examples of simple data structures such as stacks and queues? Several papers showed its limitations when slight additional behavioral features are added (Majster, 1977; Bertzliss and Thatte, 1983; Guttag and Horning, 1983). For example, a stack with an internal marker eluded representation. Remedies were offered such as going to higher-order logics and introducing hidden components (Bergstra and Tucker, 1987).

Q: What led you to your solution?

A: While in Sydney, a report from Parnas' group (Parnas and Madey, 1990) came out with a trace specification of a cursored list. Although not explicitly stated, the presumption was that this could not be expressed with algebraic specifications. And, while made more understandable by the new tabular form, the trace specification of the cursored list looked highly suspect to me. It was as if a Turing Machine head were riding back and forth over the full trace of the operation history and reconstructing the information needed for the current state of the object. Why not represent this state in a more direct fashion?

Q: Why not?

A: Because if you stick with the given interface operators, this cannot be done. This and the algebraic extensions were trying to work with the given interface and as a consequence were doing a simulation of the object rather than specifying the behavior of the object itself.

Q: So the solution was to focus on complete state representation?

A: Yes, when I returned home and started teaching the material again, it finally dawned on me that the only way to make specification direct and not a simulation was to find an appropriate set of state-representing queries, even if some of them were to be hidden. That's how I came up with the specification of the list class in Chapter 3. The cursored list could then be directly represented by using the list state queries (in hidden form) and portraying the effect of motion operations on the cursor (see Problem 7 of Chapter 3). Implementation in C++ follows nicely using private inheritance (see Problem 5 of Chapter 6).

Q: What's the essential difference between your state-representing queries and traditional algebraic approaches?

A: Traditional approaches tacitly assume that commands can be partitioned into upbuilding and downbuilding subsets where the downbuilding ones can be eliminated by equations. The classic stack and queue are the prototype examples where the downbuilding pop and remove operations, respectively, are eliminated by equations that express their interplay with the upbuilding push and add commands, respectively. My approach considers such elimination as being so unlikely in general that it is not worth considering, let alone establishing as the basis of a general approach. But this only became clear after working with the systems and Nerode equivalence concepts, and giving up this form was

Objects and Systems

painful. I had to convince myself with the characterization of the list behavior (Chapter 3) and later that of the general order class (Chapter 10) that what was gained was much more valuable than what was lost since stacks and queues in my approach are not as straightforward as in the traditional one.

Going to state representation also made it important to find primitives for a behavior. In this way, the state representation, in the form of state-representing queries, would only need to support the primitives.

Q: But if complete state representation is used, why not use state-oriented specifications such as Z?

A: For two reasons. One, Z (Diller, 1990; Durnota, 1994) and other state-oriented specifications (Jones, 1986) require that the state be specified in a set theory-based notation. This fixes the state quite strongly. State-representing queries, on the other hand, specify only what the return value type is and thus still leave the actual state representation decision to the implementation.

Two, the command/query form still relates to the interface concept and also retains the form of the original algebraic specification. So it is possible to easily compute the number of state equations needed for complete specification. The syntax constraints of the algebraic approach are retained as well.

Q: Why is this syntax important?

A: It provides a crucible in which specification can be done. In fact, my students and I have implemented software that supports the specification process (Williams, 1992; Vahie, 1993). The initial input is the syntax (prototypes) of the constructor, commands, and queries. This is used to generate the set of left-hand sides of the required number of equations. The user then fills in the right-hand sides, and the software checks that the right-hand sides are syntactically correct. Of course, semantic correctness cannot be checked since the semantics are the specification itself. The software then generates test forms based on the equations along the lines of Chapter 7.

Q: Why so much focus on testing as opposed to verification?

A: Verification requires understanding of logical calculii (Woodcock and Loomes, 1988) that undergraduates don't have. Moreover, in today's state-of-the-art, it is still a difficult, error prone art that can be practiced by very few professionals. Testing, on the other hand, is more direct and intuitive. Designing for testability (Binder, 1994) is possible since tests can be generated directly from the behavior specification, and this gives strong motivation to learn to do such specification. Students with this background can go on to learn refinement (Whysall and McDermid, 1994) and verification methods in later courses.

Q: You said that systems theory was the guiding light in your approach. But doesn't category theory address the same issues in more rigorous form?

A: Unfortunately, category theory (Goguen et al., 1978) adds a second layer of abstraction to what is already almost too abstract for most undergraduates. Furthermore, I feel that the Nerode behavior equivalence concept is an adequate basis for object behavior specification and its simplicity evaporates when rephrased more abstractly in category-theoretic terms.

Q: Given their importance, how are systems theory and the Nerode equivalence manifested in the book?

A: The systems concepts (Zeigler, 1976, 1990) of structure, behavior, and their interrelation are phrased directly in terms of constructors, commands, queries, state transitions, and behavior-generating simulations. This starts with their finite state manifestations and continues with the infinite state representations made possible by adopting the essentials of the syntactical forms borrowed from algebraic specification.

Q: How did the HCCL come about? Aren't container libraries common?

A: The HCCL owes much to the initiative of an enterprising undergraduate student, Lip Saw. I asked him to check if there was anything widely available in C++ that could duplicate the heterogeneous list capabilities of Lisp. Because nothing of that kind existed, he went ahead and did most of the implementation, documentation, and testing for his senior project based on the specification I developed. Incidentally, this paradigm might be good for many undergraduate senior projects or software engineering group projects.

Q: Why devote so much space to ensemble methods?

A: Ensemble methods are at the heart of the demonstration that classical iterator behavior can be specified in a manner that is neutral with respect to sequential and parallel implementations. In effect, classical iterator specification allows the characteristics of the underlying technology (sequential computing) to influence the behavior specification. The original seed of ensemble methods lay in the for-all and map forms in Scheme and Lisp. But given the complexity of the classical iterator specifications (Lamb, 1990; Shaw, 1981), I had to convince myself that the apparent simplicity of these forms was not an illusion. This eventually led to the test of expressive power set forth in Chapters 9 and 10. Could ensemble methods realize all the behavior in the container class hierarchy? It turned out that the original tell-all and ask-all methods had to be supplemented by three new ones (which?, which-one?, and reduce) to do so. This further emphasized the usefulness of seeking primitives, this time for a whole repertoire of behaviors (not just a single one). The end result, an informal proof of expressive power of the ensemble methods, shows that the same containers' behavior can be implemented in both sequential and parallel technologies. In other words, we can use object orientation to hide these technologies within container classes.

Q: And finally, why is that important?

A: Because we can develop systems based on containers by working at the specification level and delay the decision of which technology to use to the implementation phase. Also, we can have portability from sequential to parallel technologies and partition processing between sequential and parallel modes for optimal efficiency (Cho, 1994). This is the approach taken in the development of the DEVS-C++ simulation environment (Zeigler and Louri, 1990; Zeigler et al., 1996), which achieves both high-level portability and high performance.

Contents

Introduction for the Student and the Instructor

Why a Principled Approach Is Needed

Formal approaches to software development are gaining greater acceptance in practice these days. This is especially true in projects where safety is absolutely critical, such as in airplane control software, or where a software crash could cause a major foul-up such as in the telephone system. But it is also true in general as software developers strive to achieve higher levels of maturity on the Software Enterprise Institute's (SEI) scale. This is a model of achievement that is becoming widely accepted as a credential necessary to qualify to bid on a contract. So it is important that students have not only the basic programming skills but also the understanding of formal principles that enable them to fit into high SEI–ranking software organizations.

This book is based on the belief that object orientation provides a powerful way to build complex software systems. This belief is supported by the overwhelming adoption of C++ as the programming language of choice, with installations in the hundreds of thousands. Nevertheless, a programming language by itself does not provide a set of sound principles to use — you can just as easily program poorly in C++ as in its nonobject-oriented predecessor, C. Thus, this book aims to provide formal principles for object-oriented system development that guide the effective application of object-oriented programming constructs.

Technology Invariance and Skills Survival

C++ is the programming champion today, as was Fortran in the past, but it is hard to guarantee that it will remain so in 10 years. Technology today is moving toward networked and distributed computing, and this will certainly influence the programming-language standard. Today we can already see the rise of Java, the object-oriented language for World Wide Web programming. But standards and specifications are more permanent than languages and technologies. We can see this as the premise underlying the effort to define a Common Object Request Broker Architecture (CORBA). This effort, supported by many of the world's leading information age companies, is to provide workable specifications that will enable objects to interact by adhering to common interfaces while hiding the details of their implementations (vendors, languages, technologies, and so on.)

But principles are even more permanent than specifications. So the concepts we present here, while shown to work in C++ and Java, are also aimed at future languages, technologies and systems that are likely to be distributed, parallel and global. They will help you surf with the waves of technology change that can be expected in the next century.

Toward a Disciplined Realistic Software Development Process

What distinguishes the principled programming process of the book from current practice? A series of diagrams will suggest the answer. Figure 1 depicts our natural programming tendencies. There are three steps:

1. conceptualize: think about the problem.
2. write code: express your ideas directly in programming form.
3. debug: execute and modify the code until it does what you want.

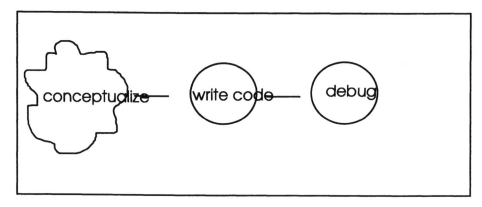

Figure 1. Common programming practice.

On the other hand, software engineering texts prescribe methodologies for software development that are much more disciplined. Figure 2 illustrates our version of such a methodology. According to it, you should

1. conceptualize: think about the desired behavior of the software.
2. specify: express the behavior exactly.
3. concurrently
   • implement: write code that realizes the desired behavior,

- develop test plan: design tests that reveal whether the code actually does realize the desired behavior.
4. debug: correct the flaws revealed by the tests until the tests are all satisfied.

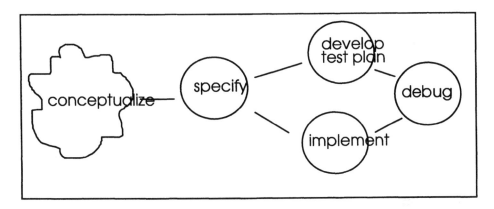

Figure 2 Idealized software development process

This scenario imagines that you can think through all of the situations encountered by the software application and determine what it is expected to do in each. Having done this, you can proceed to implement the system in coded form. Now, since the desired behavior has been defined precisely, tests can be developed based on it before actual implementation. So after both have been completed, the tests are executed on the implemented system. This can be called a "waterfall model" since the work progresses downstream with no reversals.

The waterfall model has, alas, become the model that methodologists love to hate. Ordinary people just can't practice what it preaches, and numerous amendments to it have been proposed that are more in keeping with what humans can do. Nevertheless, the individual phases it identifies are essential to the principled development of object oriented software. However, rather than require that they be carried out in rigid order, we view the situation as in Figure 3. We are constantly conceptualizing the problem, getting a better understanding of it, as we iterate through the phases. You may not succeed in exactly specifying the desired behavior at first, but this attempt puts you in a much better position to implement the code since you have a well-thought-out blueprint to guide you. When you develop the test plan based on the specification, you may notice some things wrong with it: nothing prevents you from going back and modifying the specification accordingly. The same goes for revisiting any of the phases. Having a good test plan makes the process of debugging much more efficient than the conventional way of doing it and makes the resulting software much more reliable.

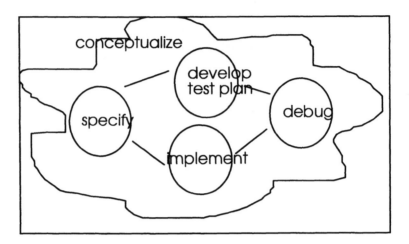

Figure 3 More realistic software development process

This book will help you understand how to carry out each of the circled tasks in Figure 3 and to appreciate why this approach is better in terms of improved software development and, just as importantly, in terms of the increased longevity of your software skills.

Objects and Systems Concepts

Some of the concepts to be developed are associated with the specification, implementation, and test plan tasks:

- specify behavior:
  ◊ objects
  ◊ states
  ◊ constructors, queries, commands
  ◊ state equations
- implement:
  ◊ classes
  ◊ inheritance
  ◊ hierarchical construction
  ◊ class reuse
- develop test plan:
  ◊ convert state equations to tests
  ◊ coverage
  ◊ efficiency

◊   test reuse

These concepts merge two streams of ideas. Object orientation provides an operational level tool kit that supports effective software development. However, the framework that provides the guiding light to achieve such effectiveness is that of systems theory—specifically, its concepts of state and behavior, and of hierarchical system construction.

We'll demonstrate the methodology by designing a library of container classes, that is, classes that work like lists to hold objects. Furthermore, these classes, called the Heterogeneous Container Class Library (HCCL), will be built with features that enable them to be reused again and again in the construction of complex systems. And we will show how they can be implemented in the parallel/distributed technologies on the horizon. So it will be worth understanding their behavior, from the specifications given, independently of their implementation.

Teaching and Learning

This book is intended as a text offering a semiformal, principled introduction to object-oriented software design and application system programming. The presentation is focused at the level of junior/senior (third or fourth year) undergraduates in computer science and engineering. While all the elements of C++ necessary to understand the approach are provided, the book should be supplemented with a manual or programming-level exposition of C++ to supply further mechanical details, such as how to invoke the compiler, how to write make-files, and so on. The presentation assumes a modest background in programming and acquaintance with data structures. Although C++ is the primary vehicle for illustrating the concepts, other languages also appear. Scheme and Lisp are mentioned in some of the problems. The last chapter illustrates the major concepts in the Web programming language, Java.

A course based on the book should serve as a prerequisite to a full-scale software engineering course. As object orientation takes firmer root, many computer science and engineering subfields will be taught from an object-oriented perspective with C++ (or other OO language) software. In this scenario, a course based on this book would become a prerequisite to many such courses.

The student will be unfamiliar with the concepts, but very likely, the instructor will be too. Seeing examples of applications before getting down to hard work should provide the motivation to move forward. However, a book must have a logical order where the content precursors of any instruction unit precede its presentation. Hence, complex, realistic examples appear at the end only when all the tools have been developed. But there is nothing to prevent teaching and learning in a more holistic style—suitably distilling the gist of later material to motivate the groundwork that must be understood first. For example, every implementation should be tested. So the test methods in Chapter 7 can be introduced, and practiced, piecemeal after the discussion of specification in Chapter 2. Both instructor and student are encouraged to mix and match from all parts of the book as needed.

Web Access

Access to further information and source code is provided on my research group's World Wide Web site: http\\:www-ais.ece.arizona.edu. This site also features advanced application of HCCL to discrete event modeling environments that support both serial and parallel/distributed simulation. Please surf to the Web site to discover how powerful the concepts developed in this book really are!

Bibliography

M. A. Arbib, *Theories of Abstract Automata.* Prentice–Hall, Englewood Cliffs, NJ, 1969.

A. Bergstra and J. V. Tucker, "Algebraic Specifications of Computable and Semicomputable Data Types," *Theoretical Computer Science*, Vol. 50, pp. 137–181, 1987.

A.T. Bertzliss and S. Thatte, "Specification and Implementation of Abstract Data Types." In *Advances in Computers*, Vol. 22, Academic Press, NY, 1983.

R. Binder, "Design for Testability in Object Oriented Systems," *Comm.of the ACM*, Vol. 37, no. 9, 1994.

G. Booch, *Object-Oriented Design with Applications.* Benjamin/Cummings, Redwood City, CA, 1991.

T. Budd, *An Introduction to Object-Oriented Programming.* Addison Wesley, Reading, MA, 1991

L. Cardelli and P. Wegner, "On Understanding Types, Data Abstraction, and Polymorphism," *ACM Computing Surveys*, Vol. 17 no. 4, pp. 471–522, 1985.

Y. Cho, Parallel Implementation of Containers in PVM. Master's Thesis, ECE Dept., U. Arizona, 1994.

P. Coad and E. Yourdon, *Object–Oriented Analysis*, Prentice–Hall, Berlin, 1991.

A. Diller, *Z: An Introduction to Formal Methods.* John Wiley, New York, 1990.

B. Durnota, "Defining relationships in Ecology Using Object–Oriented Formal Specifications," *Math. Comp. Modeling*, Vol. 20, no. 8, pp. 83–96, 1994.

R. Failey, *Software Engineering Concepts*, McGraw-Hill, New York, 1985.

N. Y. Foo, "Algebraic Specifications as Solutions of Implementation Equations," *IEEE Trans. Soft. Engr.*, Vol. SE–13, no. 12. pp. 465–470, Dec. 1987.

J. A. Goguen, J. W. Thatcher and E. G. Wagner, "An Initial Algebra Approach to the Specification, Correctness, and Implementation of Abstract Data Types." pp. 80–149. In *Current Trends in Programming Methodology, Vol. 4: Data Structuring*, ed. R. T. Yeh, Prentice-Hall, Englewood Cliffs, NJ, 1978.

J. V. Guttag and J.J. Horning, "The Algebraic Specification of Datatypes." *Acta Inform.*, Vol. 10, pp. 97–121, Jan. 1983.

C. B. Jones, *Systematic Software Development using VDM*, Prentice-Hall, Englewood Cliffs, NJ, 1986.

D. A. Lamb, *Software Engineering, Planning for Change*, Prentice-Hall, Englewood Cliffs, NJ, 1988.

D.A. Lamb, "Specification of Iterators." *IEEE Trans. Software Engineering*, Vol. 16, no. 12, pp. 1352–1360, 1990.

B. Liskov and J. Guttag, *Abstraction and Specification in Program Development.* MIT Press, Cambridge, MA, 1986.

E. Majster, "Limits of the Algebraic Specification of Data Types." *ACM SIGPLAN Notices*, Vol. 12, no. 10, pp. 97–121, Oct. 1977.

B. Meyer, *Object–Oriented Software Construction.* Prentice-Hall, Englewood Cliffs, NJ., 1988.

B. Meyer, "On Formalism in Specification." *IEEE Software*, Vol. 2, No. 1, pp. 6–26, 1985.

B. Meyer, *Eifel: The Language,* Prentice-Hall, NJ, 1992.

D. L. Parnas and J. Madey, Function Documentation for Computer Systems Engineering. Tech. Rep. 90–287, TRIO, Queen's University, Kingston, Ontario, September 1990.

D. L. Parnas and P. C. Clements, "A Rational Design Process: How and Why to Fake It", *IEEE Trans. on Soft. Eng.*, Vol. SE–12, No. 2, 251–257. February, 1986.

H. Saiedian and many others, "An Invitation to Formal Methods", IEEE Computer, April 1996, Vol. 29, No. 4, pp. 16–32.

G. Scott Owen, M. D. Fraser, and R. A. Gagliano, "Knowledge Based Tools for Reusable ADA Software." In *Empirical Foundations of Information and Software Science V*, eds. P. Zunde and D. Hocking, Plenum Press, NY, 1986.

M. Shaw, *Alphard: Form and Content.* Springer-Verlag, New York, 1981.

M. Stefik and D. G. Bobrow, "Object–Oriented Programming: Themes and Variations." *AI Magazine*, pp. 40–62, Winter, 1986.

B. Stroustrup, "What is Object–Oriented Programming?" *IEEE Software*, Vol. 5, no. 3, pp. 10–20, 1989.

J. W. Thatcher, E.G. Wagner and J. B. Wright, Data Type Specification: Parametrization and the Power of Specification Techniques. IBM Research Report RC 7757, Yorktown Heights, NY, 1979.

S. Vahie, Axiomatic Specification of Composite Object Behaviors. Master's Thesis, ECE Dept. U. Arizona, 1993.

P. Wegner, "Dimensions of Object–Oriented modelling." *IEEE Computer,* pp. 12–20, 1992.

P.J. Whysall and J. A. McDermid, *Object-Oriented Specification and Refinement.* Fourth Refinement Workshop, Springer-Verlag, New York, pp. 150–184, 1994,

G. Wilkie, *Object-Oriented Software Engineering,* Addison–Wesley, Reading, MA, 1995.

B. E. Williams, An incremental Development system for axiom Specified Objects. Master's Thesis, ECE Dept., U. Arizona, 1992.

J. Woodcock and M. Loomes, *Software Engineering Mathematics*, Addison Wesley, Reading, MA, 1988.

A.W. *Wymore A Mathematical Theory of Systems Engineering: The Elements*, John Wiley, NY, 1967.

B.P. Zeigler, *Theory of Modelling and Simulation*, John Wiley, New York, 1976.

B.P. Zeigler. *Object–Oriented Simulation with Hierarchical, Modular Models: Intelligent Agents and Endomorphic Systems.* Academic Press, NY, 1990.

B. P. Zeigler and N. Foo, "Nerode–Based Theory of Object Specification and Realization", submitted to *IEEE Trans. Software Engineering* (1991, still in review process!)

B. P. Zeigler and A. Louri, "A Simulation Environment for Intelligent Machine Architecture." *Journal of Par. and Dist. Proc,* Vol. 16, no. 12, 1990.

B. P. Zeigler, Y. Moon, D. H. Kim, and J. K Kim, "DEVS–C++: An Environment for High Performance Simulation", *Procs. of the Hawaii Intl. Conf. on Systems Science*, 1996.

1
Object Orientation and State Systems

This chapter uses simple state machines to introduce the basic concepts of object orientation. You have run across state-system concepts in earlier courses, such as discrete math. One immediate advantage of using such concepts is that they enable us to describe the functioning of an object in a form independent of any particular software implementation. Using state diagrams, we can specify what functionality we want to obtain and then investigate different ways to achieve it. One of the simplest, yet nontrivial, examples of a finite state machine is the binary counter. First we implement this machine in C using a nonobject-oriented implementation. Then we will show how this machine can be implemented in C++. This will provide the basis for comparing the two kinds of approaches to programming and thereby demonstrate the advantages of object orientation.

1.1 Finite State Machine Example: Binary Counter

When the binary counter is fed a sequence of 0s and 1s it responds with a predictable sequence of 0s and 1s. The 1s in the output stream occur at every alternate occurrence of a 1 in the input sequence. A *state/output diagram* for the binary counter is given in Figure 1. Note that 0 inputs never affect the state or output of the system; 1 inputs cause the machine to cycle back and forth between states 0 and 1. The only time the machine emits a nonzero output is when it is transitioning from the 1 state to the 0 state.

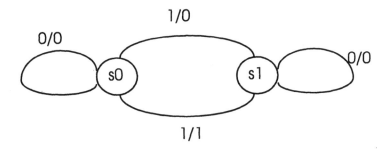

Figure 1. State/output of a binary counter.

Binary Counter: Nonobject-Oriented Implementation

Figure 2 shows how we might implement this behavior in C, the non-object oriented predecessor of C++. To experiment with this device, we might "inject" a series of 1's and 0's and display the outputs (the arrow "→" stands for "prints out"; it is not a part of C++ language):

```
printf("1d",output(1)); → 0
transition(1);

printf("1d",output(1)); → 1
transition(1);

printf("1d",output(1)); → 0
transition(1);

printf("1d",output(1)); → 1
transition(1);

printf("1d",output(1)); → 0
transition(1);

printf("1d",output(1)); → 1
transition(1);
```

Note that every second input of 1 results in an output of 1, as required. An input sequence of all zeros produces the same sequence as output. This is true no matter what state we left the counter in. Try it.

There is an important constraint we have to observe in writing test sequences such as that above. We first *query* for output with a particular input and then issue a *command* for a transition with the same input. Technically, this is called a *Mealy* machine (after a pioneer in computer science). In such a device, the input causes an output and a state transition at the same time. It would be inconsistent, for example, to request our implementation to output its response to an input 0 and then give it a 1 input to make a state transition.

```
int state = 0;

void reset(){
state = 0;
}

int output (int inp){
if (state == 0)
    return 0;
else if ( inp == 1)
    return 1;
    else return 0;
}

void transition (int inp){
  if (inp == 1) {
    if (state == 0)
      state = 1;
    else
      state = 0;
    }
}
```

Figure 2. Code for implementing the binary counter.

Rather than remember this constraint, we can combine the query and command procedures into one procedure and use it instead:

```
int outputTHENtransition (inp){
int save = output(inp);
transition( inp);
return save;
)
```

Using this new composite procedure we can inject an input sequence such as 110 this way:

```
printf("1d",outputTHENtransition (1));
printf("1d",outputTHENtransition (1));
printf("1d",outputTHENtransition (0));
```

1.2 Problems with Nonobject-Oriented Programming

Having introduced the implementation of the binary counter in C puts us in a position to point out some of the problems that occur in non object-oriented programming. After examining these problems, we will develop an object-oriented implementation of the same device. This will allow us to demonstrate some of the software development advantages of object-oriented programming,

The following problems are easily identified in the binary counter implementation.

Everything is Exposed

Defining the output and transition procedures separately is good because it allows us to define and test each of these aspects of the device separately. Such separation is always the best approach to getting an implementation to work properly. Moreover, combining the two procedures into one achieves the final goal of the implementation, namely to be able to input sequences and get the proper output sequences. However, having defined output and transition for our own scaffolding purposes, we really would not like to expose them to end users. They might, after all, forget the constraint and create an inconsistency between state and output (blaming us for it when its effect surfaces). There is no way to do this unless we can somehow encapsulate the implementation and expose only a portion, (i.e., output-THEN transition), leaving the rest hidden to the user. Such encapsulation and information hiding is one important feature offered by object-oriented systems. Let's look at other problems with our C implementation that are readily solved with object orientation.

Unrestricted Global Access

There is no way in the C implementation to prevent the end user or some other part of a program from tampering with the internal state of the counter. For example, suppose that the statement

    reset();

appears somewhere in a program; and somewhere else — possibly far removed — output-THENtransition is invoked:

    outputTHENtransition(1);

Now suppose that further on in the code, the state is directly altered:

    state = 0;

Since the state is not what it should be, a second invocation of outputTHENtransition(1) encounters a wrong state and yields a wrong output: 0 instead of 1. Tracking down where this invalid assignment was made can be excruciatingly difficult. After all, we might have to look through the whole program (and there could be millions of lines of code in a modern software system) to find the source of the error.

The problem in this implementation is that state is a ***global variable***—any user (person or procedure) can change it at will. What we want is for only ***inputs*** and, possibly, ***intentional resets***, to be able to change this state. So what we need is a way to encapsulate the state within an interface that channels access to the hidden variables through intentionally specified queries and commands.

No Convenient Replication

In real hardware design, power-of-two counters (able to count up to 4, 8, 16,...) are made by cascading binary counters together, feeding the output of one as the input to the next. Each successive counter sees exactly half as many 1s as its predecessor. So a 1 will appear at the output of a cascade of two counters for every four input 1s, a cascade of three counters will output a 1 for every eight input 1s, and so on. To mimic this hardware approach, we need to be able to replicate device implementations at will. However, our current implementation makes this rather tedious to do.

One approach, for example, is to rewrite the same code with distinct variable and procedure names for each counter we need. For instance:

```
int state1 = 0;

void reset1(){
state1= 0;
}
...
```

and so on. Then to inject a 1 to a counter and feed its output to a successor, we can write

```
int y = outputTHEN transition(1);
outputTHEN transition1(y);
```

Since we are not interested in the intermediate result itself, we could just as well write

```
outputTHEN transition1 (outputTHEN transition(1))}
```

An input sequence of four 1s would cause a final 1 output as required for a four-counter:

```
printf(" 1d",outputTHENtransition1(outputTHEN transition (1))) = 0
printf(" 1d",outputTHENtransition1(outputTHEN transition (1))) = 0
printf(" 1d",outputTHENtransition1(outputTHEN transition (1))) = 0
printf(" 1d",outputTHENtransition1(outputTHEN transition (1))) = 1
```

Of course using a text editor cuts down the tedium involved in copying code. But this is still not a very reliable or elegant way to do things. Object orientation provides the proper basis for such replication.

1.3 Benefits of Object Orientation: Binary Counter
C++ Implementation

How does object orientation solve the replication, exposure, and access problems just discussed? An *object-oriented programming system (OOPS)* is built around the concepts of **object** — a package of data and procedures, and **classes** — templates for generating such objects. In its simplest form, a class definition specifies the fields, called *data members* (also called *instance variables*), and the procedures, called the *function members* (also called *methods*) that each of its instances will have. Figure 3 contains a class definition in C++ for the binary counter .

Having made such a definition, we can create instances—objects with these instance variables and methods—at will using *constructors,* illustrated in Figure 4.

In the program's environment, the global variable bc1 is now bound to the instance of binary counters just created. This means that bc1 has all the properties accorded to any instance of class binary counters—in this case, this means having a slot called state . Any other instance of binary counters, say bc2, that we choose to make would also have a slot called state. But since they are encapsulated in different objects, bc1 and bc2, these fields are completely independent of each other. To verify this, we can initialize two instances with different states:

```
binary_counter bc1(0);
binary_counter bc2(1);
```

We can apply the methods declared in the class declaration to any instance of binary_counter. This is done through message passing. For example, to send a message to bc1 to reset:

```
bc1.reset();
```

Examine the code in the methods in Figure 3. You will notice that it looks exactly like the code in our original, nonobject-oriented implementation. However, in this case, the same code suffices for each and every instance that we wish to create — when a message is sent to an instance, its own environment is used to interpret that message. Thus the same message sent to bc1 produces a different response than it does to bc2 when they are in different states.

```
class binary_counter { // define a class called binary_counter

private:      // the following are private to the class
        // (discussed in text)

  int state; // declare state as an instance variable of
          // type integer
  int output (int input) { // define output as a query method
    if (input == 0)
      return 0;
    else if (state == 0)
      return 0;
    else
      return 1;

  }

void transition (int input) { // define transition as a command
                  // method (shown by declaring void as
                  // its return value)
  if (input == 1) {
    if (state == 0)
      state = 1;
    else
      state = 0;
    }
  }

public: // the following are public (explained in text)

binary_counter(){ state = 0; }  // define a constructor for
                  // a class

binary_counter(int initial_state) { // here is another choice
                  // of class constructor

state = initial_state;
  }

  void reset() { state = 0; }
  int outputTHENtransition(int input) {
    int out = output(input); // declare local integer variable
                  // called out and give it the value
                  // computed by output
    transition(input);

    return out;

  }

}; // end the class declaration
```

Figure 3. C++ class definition for binary counter.

```
// two ways in which class instances can be created
// are illustrated:


binary_counter bc1 = binary_counter(0);//declares and defines
                    //bc1 at the same time

binary_counter bc2(0); // short form for achieving
                // the previous result

// an alternative form of creating an instance is to
// first declare a pointer to it:

binary_counter * bcp;

// the actual instance is constructed using the general
// constructor new:

bcp = new binary_counter(0);

// this can be combined into one step:

binary_counter * bcp = new binary_counter(0);
```

Figure 4. Illustrating constructors in C++.

```
// the following invoke the outputTHENtransition methods
// for bc1 and bc2, respectively:

cout <<
  "output of bc1 is:"<< bc1.outputTHENtransition(0)
      << endl;
cout << "output of bc2 is : "
    << bc2.outputTHENtransition(1) << endl;
```

As before, we can send the output of bc1 to the input of bc2:

```
bc2.outputTHENtransition(bc1.outputTHENtransition(0)) ;
```

When referencing a pointer to an instance, rather than the instance itself, the arrow (->) replaces the dot (.). For example, having constructed bcp in Figure 4, we can send messages such as:

```
bcp->outputTHENtransition(0);
bcp->outputTHENtransition(1);
bcp->reset();
```

1.4 Access Restrictions in C++

C++ makes a distinction between *public* and *private* access specifications in its class declarations. Both data and function members may be declared as public or private (*protected* is another possibility, which will be discussed later). A *private* member can be accessed only within an instance environment; a *public* member can be accessed in any environment. Declaring a data member to be *public* makes it accessible for both reading and writing using the *dot* or *arrow* notation. In the binary counter, we want the state to be hidden within the encapsulated object, so we declare it to be *private*. Had we declared state to be *public*, its value could be obtained and altered anywhere; for example,

```
int x = bc1.state;
bc1.state = x + 1;
```

This would leave us vulnerable to the same problems of global access in nonobjected-oriented programming that we encountered earlier.

In our class declaration, the methods output and transition were declared to be private. This achieves our objective of restricting these methods to be used only within the *public* method, outputTHENtransition. Recall that this approach ensures that output and transition cannot be called independently with different inputs. The effect of declaring a variable to be public can be achieved by defining methods to access its value. These are called *accessors* in object-oriented parlance. For example, instead of declaring state as public, we can define the two accessor methods:

```
public:

int get_state() { return state };
void set_state(int val) { state = val; };
```

Note, however, the essential difference: by leaving state as public, we have the choice of not defining one or both of these accessor methods. Thus, in C++ we can allow read access to an instance variable while still preventing any inadvertent modification of it. How? Think about it before looking below!

```
private:

int state 0;

public:

int get_state() { return state };
```

This defines get_state to access state while omitting set_state (which would enable modifying state) from the class declaration. In general, the **state** of an object refers to the assignment of values to its instance variables. The only means to observe or modify the state is to apply the methods of an object (send it the appropriate message). Get_state and output are examples of so-called query methods that return views of the internal state. Set_state and transition are examples of so-called *command* methods that cause changes in state. Often methods such as outputTHENtransition contain both query and command components.

1.5 Instance Generation, Information Hiding, and Restricted Access in OOPS

Summarizing the lessons learned from the examples just discussed:

- OOPS provides class declaration facilities that enable any number of *instances* to be generated (subject only to memory limitations), each having the same *instance variables* and *methods*.
- Instances may transition between different states over time and may differ from each other in state at any time; the *state* of an object refers to the values assigned to its instance variables.
- Methods, called *queries*, of a class are the only means by which the states of its instances can be viewed; the class designer can hide the internals of the object and expose only those aspects that are consistent with the "advertised" behavior.
- Methods, called *commands*, of a class are the only means by which the states of its instances can be altered; the class designer can thus restrict changes to instance variables to only those aspects that are consistent with the "advertised" behavior.
- Instance variables and methods can be hidden from public exposure by declaring them to be private.

Problems

1.

(a) An n-counter generalizes the concept of binary counter—it counts up to n−1 before returning to state 0. Along the way it outputs 0's until the transition from n−1 to 0. Define a class of n-counters, where n, a positive integer, is a parameter of the class (it is supplied an argument to the class constructor). Implement the class in C++.

(b) Build a class of four-counters by using two slots to hold binary counters and then have the first send output to the second; the output produced is that of the second binary counter. Implement the class in C++.

(c) In view of (a) and (b) how many ways are there to implement an n-counter, for given n?

2. Define a class bank-accts in C++. There are two command methods: deposit and withdraw, each with a single argument, called amount. There is an instance variable called balance. Deposits of positive amounts can always be done. Withdrawals can only be done if the requested amount is covered by the balance. Study the following properties of OO programming in this context:

- *replication*: open several accounts with different initial balances.
- *restricted exposure:* suppose that a friend is not told how an account was initialized. Can she find out what the balance is? To rectify this situation, add a query: balance? that returns the balance in the account.
- *restricted access*: even though an account's balance can now be obtained, can it be altered other than through the deposit and withdraw methods?

Suppose you were trying to "break-into" an account. Could you do so?

3. A finite state machine that keeps track of whether a variable has been set is shown below. It starts with the variable undefined. When the variable is set, it goes to the defined state. An attempt to set the variable again is illegal until a clear has changed the state back to undefined.

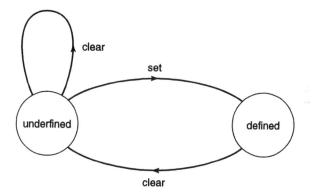

Implement this machine in C++ as a class def. Create at least two distinct instances of this class and show how the effect of a set command is different in different states.

2
Object Behavior Specification: Software Blueprints

It may be difficult to imagine yourself simultaneously playing the roles of designer, implementor, tester, and user of a software tool. But that's what best describes your activities if you are writing a program for your own later use. When you graduate, you might participate in a software development team where it is now common that designer, implementor, tester, and other roles are assumed by specialists on the team. For now, let's stick with the case where you are the designer, implementer, tester and user of a software tool. Some form of abstract specification of the software is needed to facilitate communication among designer, implementor, and user. We will call it a *blueprint* (playing the same role as design sketches used by building architects) as illustrated in Figure 1. Suppose you are developing a set of classes in C++ or some other object-oriented language.

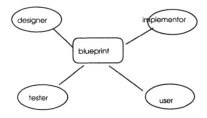

Figure 1. The mediating role of a software blueprint.

- As *designer* you should create a blueprint to provide the **implementor** (yourself) with clear guide lines on the code to be written.
- As *tester*, you should use the blueprint to develop your tests for correctness (i.e., to see if the classes realize the desired behavior).
- Later, as *user*, you will be glad to have the blueprint around when you have forgotten how to use some of the features that were obvious to you when you were in the development stage.

While needed by an individual developer such as yourself, such a blueprint is essential in a software team setting. Without it, the implementor and tester can't be sure what the designer has in mind, and later the user may not be able to find out enough about the available features of the software to make it useful. Indeed, a less detailed, more readable form of the blueprint can be used to document the functionality in the form of a user's manual.

We have already seen an example of a *language-independent* specification: the finite state diagrams for the binary counter in Chapter 1. This chapter will acquaint you more fully with what an object behavior specification should provide, enable you to understand such specifications, and even help you write some.

2.1 Object Behavior Specification

There are many forms that an object behavior specification can take, including state diagrams, tables, or statements in an appropriate logical calculus. However, we will standardize on one form in most of this book. In this section, we outline the form that this specification will take. Don't be put off if the form doesn't fully make sense at first. You can return to it for reference as you come across examples throughout the book.

Here is the form of an object behavior specification:

- **class**, the name of the class of objects to be specified:
- **constructors**, one or more procedures to create instances of the class:
- **queries**, methods that return values without changing the state of an object; we may also designate methods as *hidden* (corresponds to private in C++).:
- **commands**, methods that may change the state and do not return values:
- **domain restrictions,** which describe the restrictions governing method application;
- **equivalences** are the relationships that specify the behavior of the class instances; there are two main types: *state equations* and *definitions*. The number of state equations needed for a complete specification depends directly on the number of queries, constructors and commands (Figure 2):

Number of state equations =

    Number of State Representing Queries

$$\times$$

    Number of Constructors + Number of Commands

Reason: each query must be paired with each constructor and command

---

Figure 2. Number of state equations.

Example of Object Behavior Specification: Combination Lock

We will write a behavior specification for a class of combination locks that will function like real padlocks. Our first step is to form a model of a padlock (Figure 3).

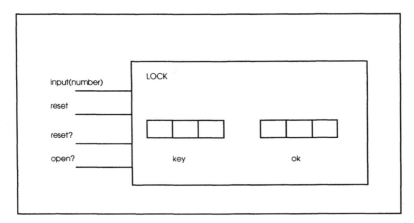

Figure 3. A combination lock.

There is a definite sequence of steps that must be performed in order to open such a lock. First, the dial must be rotated fully three times to establish the proper initial conditions. Thus in our model, there is a method to reset the lock. There is a combination, a sequence of three numbers, that when matched in the given order by rotations releases the catch and opens the lock. In our model there are 3 numbers to hold the combination, called the *key* vector. There is a vector, ok, of 3 corresponding boolean variables that record progress toward the goal. To represent the rotations of the dial, we send input messages to the lock object. If, after resetting the lock, the first input matches the first key then the first ok becomes T. Similarly, if the first ok is T and the second input matches the second key, then the second ok becomes T. Finally, if the second ok is T and the third input matches the third key, then the third ok becomes T. The lock opens when the third ok is T.

As with all English-language descriptions or requirements, there are two major difficulties:

- **ambiguity**—there is more than one way to interpret the description, and
- **incompleteness**—the description omits eventualities that can occur. (By Murphy's Law, if a problem can occur, then it will occur).

We need ways to specify desired behavior which are understandable, leave no room for ambiguity, and cover all possible conditions encountered in an object's operation. Ambiguity is always present, and you have no doubt experienced it many times when given a program to write. Incompleteness occurs when only some of the conditions of the object's behavior have been considered. For example, the above description does not specify what happens when after inputting one or two correct entries, the following entry is incorrect. Does the lock just continue to wait patiently while you continue trying to find the right number? Or does the lock reset itself immediately after the first bad attempt and oblige you to start over from scratch?

Figure 4 displays a specification of the combination lock's behavior that can serve as the blueprint concept that was just introduced.[1]

According to our model, key and phase are part of the state vector. Phase changes as inputs commands come in. In contrast, key is a parameter—it is not affected by inputs. However, we need to know the particular key of each lock instance to describe its behavior. In order to properly represent the state of the lock, we define the queries – key? and phase? to correspond to key and phase in the model. Since we need to know whether the lock is reset or not to predict its behavior, one more query, reset?, is added in. Another query, open?, reveals whether the lock opens when the complete, correct sequence of inputs has been injected. However, it is not included in the state since its value is entirely determined by phase?.

Now to write a *behavior specification*, we need to write one equation for each paired combination of queries and {constructors, commands} (of course, typically this equation breaks into several cases). Since there are

3 queries: {phase?, key?, reset?}

and

1 constructor {make-lock} + **2 commands:** {reset, input},

the **number** of equations is **3 x 3 = 9**

Figure 5 displays them. Note that where multiple cases are distinguished, such as for the combination (phase?,input) on the bottom of Figure 4, the rules (condition, action pairs) are applied in sequential order. Note that the last rule is the default, which applies whenever none of the previous ones do. Here, this states that there is no effect of input on the phase? query when a wrong *key* element is tried. In other words, an unlimited amount of experimentation is allowed—only patience is needed to exhaust all the possibilities.

---

[1] The specification employs class list to be discussed in the next chapter. For ease of explanation, we assume we can make a list from three numbers list(number1, number2, number3) and lookup the ith one using list-ref(list,i), also written as list(i).

lock

constructor

lock make-lock(number1,number2,number3)

queries

boolean open?(lock)
boolean reset?(lock)

hidden

list key?(lock)
phase phase?(lock) // for simplicity we use phase? instead of ok

commands

lock' reset(lock)
lock' input(lock,number)

Equivalences

open?(lock) = (phase?(lock) = 3)

// reset? applied after make-lock, reset, and input

reset?(make-lock(number1,number2,number3) = F

reset?(reset(lock)) = T
reset?(input(lock,number)) = F // not reset as soon
                        // as an input occurs

Figure 4. Blueprint specification of combination lock.

```
// key? applied after make-lock,reset, and input

key?(make-lock(number1,number2,number3))
            list(number1,number2,number3)

// the key is a parameter
// determined at construction

key?(reset(lock)) = key?(lock)
key?(input(lock,number)) = key?(lock)

// phase? applied after make-lock,reset
phase?(make-lock(number1,number2,number3))= 3  // lock starts open
phase?(reset(lock)) = 0 // reset also closes lock

// phase? applied after input; this breaks down into several cases;
// "rules" are applied in the given order; the first to be
// satisfied is applied

phase?(lock) = 0  & number= key?(lock)(0)
=> phase?(input(lock,number)) = 1
phase?(lock) = 1  & number= key?(lock)(1)
=> phase?(input(lock,number)) = 2
phase?(lock) = 2 & number= (key?(lock)(2)
=> phase?(input(lock,number )) = 3
phase?(input(lock,number)) = phase?(lock)
```

Figure 4 (Cont'd).

Clearly, this interpretation of combination lock logic is unambigous, but it is also not consistent with real padlock properties. Figure 5 displays an alternative specification that requires the key elements to be entered in the exact sequence of length 3. If any one is entered incorrectly, the user must reset the lock before trying again.

```
reset?(input(lock,number)) = F \ \  reset becomes false as soon
                        \ \  as an input occurs

... \ \ same as before

phase?(input(lock,number )) =  0 \ \ default case that forces
                        \ \  the user to start again
                        \ \  after missing a key element
```

Figure 5. Alternative specification preventing trial and error.

2.2 Simulating an Object Behavior Specification

The two alternative specifications for the combination lock can be used to simulate the behavior of the lock. For example, the following sequence represents a successful attempt to open the lock:

sequence 1

lock = make-lock(number1,number2,number3)

open?(lock) -> T

lock' = reset(lock)

open?(lock') -> F

lock'' = input(lock', key?(lock')(1))

open?(lock'') -> F

lock''' = input(lock'',key?(lock'')(2))

open?(lock''') -> F

lock'''' = input(lock''',key?(lock''')(3))

open?(lock'''') -> T

We can use the state equations to compute the responses to the queries shown. This works because using the equations, the state of the lock can be updated after each command. This is so because this state is represented by the query responses to the command. For example, the following is a complete simulation of the successful interaction given above:

lock = make-lock(number(3))

open?(lock) = (phase?(lock) = 3)

    = (phase?(make-lock()) = 3) = T

lock' = reset(lock)

open?(lock')

 = (phase?(lock') = 3)
 = (phase?(reset(lock)) = 3) = F
lock'' = input(lock', key?(lock')(1))
phase? (lock'')
= phase?(input(lock', key(1)?(lock')))
= 1

open?(lock'') = F

lock''' = input(lock'',key?(lock'')(2))

...
 open?(lock''') = F
 lock ^{iv} = input(lock''',key?(lock''') (3))
...
open?(lock ^{iv}) = T

The following sequence shows how "experimentation" can occur in the first specification.

sequence 2

lock = make-lock(number1,number2,number3)

open?(lock) = T

lock' = reset(lock)

open?(lock) = F

lock''= input(lock', number = key?(lock'), (1))

open?(lock'') = F

lock'''= input(lock'',number != key?(lock''), (2))

open?(lock''') = F

lock ^{iv}'= input(lock'',number = key?(lock''') (2))

open?(lock'''') = F

Using the second specification, here is a simulation of the same sequence that shows how experimentation is prevented:

```
lock = make-lock()
open?(lock) = (phase?(lock) = 3) = (phase?(make-lock()) = 3) = T
lock' = reset(lock)
open?(lock) = (phase?(lock) = 3) =
    (phase?(reset(lock)) = 3)
    = F
lock'' = input(lock' ,key?(lock') (1))
phase? (lock'') = phase?(input(lock' ,key?(lock') (1)))
    = 2

    lock = input(lock''',number != key?(lock''') (2))

    phase? (lock'') = phase?(input(lock' ,key?(lock') (1)))

    = 2

open?(lock iv) = F
reset?(lock v) = F // no further progress is possible until // the lock is reset
```

Note that each step in the simulation can, and must, be justified by an equivalence in the specification. We could have identified these justifications with comments at each step, but these were omitted in the interests of readability. However, to convince yourself of the correctness of a simulation, you should be able to write down the equivalences that justify each of its steps.

2.3 Definition of Behavior

Note that there is a query, open? after each command in the foregoing sequences. However, since queries don't change the state, they have no effect other than to provide responses. This means that the complete behavior of an object can be represented by its responses to all possible *query-terminated sequences* of commands, such as the following:

query-terminated sequence 1:

```
lock = make-lock(number(3))
open?(lock)
```

query-terminated sequence 2:

```
lock = make-lock(number(3))
lock' = reset(lock)
open?(lock')
```

query-terminated sequence 3:

```
lock = make-lock()
lock' = reset(lock)
lock'' = input(lock', key?(lock') (1))
```

open?(lock'')

Such query-terminated sequences can be used to test the object's behavior independently of its implementation. We return to discuss behavior-based test sequences in Chapter 7 on testing methodology.

Problems

1. Implement a class of combination locks in C++ to satisfy the first behavior specification given in the text. Test your implementations with the same set of query-terminated sequences of commands. Modify your implementations to conform to the second behavior specification given in the text.

2. As it stands, the bank-acct class (Problem 2, Chapter 1) does not have the ability to allow an owner to reconcile this month's closing balance with last month's closing balance and her check-book record of transactions that have transpired during the month. Add a query record?(i) that returns the ith transaction (deposit or withdrawal) for the transactions that transpired since the last record? request. Also add a query last-balance? which returns what the balance was when the last record? was requested. Note that there are now two more queries to represent the state so the state vectors of instances must be correspondingly enhanced. In general, this means that the state vector required for implementing a desired behavior depends intimately on that behavior.

3. A house alarm system is modelling by the following object behavior specification:

constructor
alarm make-alarm(key)

queries

boolean armed?(alarm)
boolean open?(alarm)
boolean sound?(alarm)

hidden
key key?(alarm)

commands

alarm' arm(alarm,key)
alarm' disarm(alarm,key)
alarm' open(alarm)
alarm' close(alarm)

Equivalences

armed?(make-alarm(key)) = F
open?(make-alarm(key)) = F
sound?(make-alarm(key)) = F
key?(make-alarm(key)) = key

open?(alarm) = F & key?(alarm) = key =>armed?(arm(alarm,key)) = T
armed?(arm(alarm,key)) = armed?(alarm)
open?( ) = F
they?( ) = key
armed?(disarm(alarm))= F
armed?(disarm) = no charge
armed?(open(alarm))) = armed?(alarm)
armed?(close(alarm)) = armed?(alarm)

open?(arm(alarm,key)) = open?(alarm)
open?(disarm(alarm,key)) = open?(alarm)
open?(open(alarm)) = T
open?(close(alarm)) = F

sound?(arm(alarm,key)) = sound?(alarm)
open?( ) = F
key = key?(alarm) => sound?(disarm(alarm,key)) = F
sound?(disarm(alarm,key)) = sound?(alarm)
armed?(alarm) = T => sound?(open(alarm)) = T
sound?(open(alarm)) = sound?(alarm)
sound?(close(alarm)) = sound?(alarm)

key?(arm(alarm,key)) = key?(alarm)
key?(disarm(alarm,key)) = key?(alarm)
key?(open(alarm)) = key?(alarm)
key?(close(alarm)) = key?(alarm)

4. Implement this specification as a class of alarms in C++. Write some query-terminated command sequences, and use the specification to obtain the expected response associated with each sequence. Use these sequences to test the implementations.
5. Write a behavior specification for the binary counter presented in Chapter 1. Base
   your specification on current-state? as the state-representing query and output?
   as the other query, reset and transition being the commands. Note that it is difficult to write a specification in terms of outputTHENtranstion since it combines
   both a query and a command into one method.

6. Implement and test the following object behavior specification for a class of objects that provides read/write access restrictions to an encapsulated variable.

constructor
make-acc(pw-initial,value-initial)

commands
acc′ set-read(acc,pw,boolean)
acc′ set-write(acc,pw,boolean)
acc′ set-v(acc,value)

queries
boolean read?(acc)
boolean write?(acc)
value v?(acc)

hidden
pw get-pw(acc)
value get-v(acc)

Domain Restrictions

set-write(acc,pw,boolean) = defined provided that pw = get-pw(acc)
set-read(acc,pw,boolean) = defined provided that pw = get-pw(acc)
set-v(acc) = defined provided that write?(acc) = T
v?(acc) = defined provided that read?(acc) = T

Equivalences

v?(acc) = get-v(acc) // provided domain restrictions are satisfied
read?(make-acc(pw-initial,value-initial)) =T
read?(set-read(acc,pw,boolean)) = boolean
read?(set-write(acc,pw,T)) = T //write access enables read access
read?(set-write(acc,pw,F)) = read?(acc)
read?(set-v(acc,value)) = read?(acc)
write?(make-acc(pw-initial,value-initial)) =T
write?(set-write(acc,pw,boolean)) = boolean
write?(set-read(acc,pw,boolean)) = write?(acc)
write?(set-v(acc,value)) = write?(acc)

get-v(make-acc(pw-initial,value-initial)) = value-initial
get-v(set-write(acc,pw,boolean)) = get-v(acc)
get-v(set-read(acc,pw, boolean)) = get-v(acc)
get-v(set-v(acc, value)) = value

get-pw(make-acc(pw-initial,value-initial)) =pw-initial
get-pw(set-pw(acc,pw,boolean)) = pw
get-pw(set-read(acc,pw,boolean)) = get-pw(acc)
get-pw(set-v(acc,value)) = get-pw(acc)
get-pw(set-write(acc,pw,boolean)) = get-pw(acc)

3
Lists: Behavior Specification, Models and Implementations

You are familiar with linked lists from earlier courses in programming. Some languages, such as Lisp and Scheme, provide lists as built-in data structures together with some essential associated operations. But most languages don't provide lists as basic data structures, so we must create and manipulate them using their basic data-structuring and procedure definition facilities. How would we go about defining a class of list objects and methods in such a language?

Indeed, let's go one step further. Suppose that the language of interest provides object-oriented programming features. How would we define lists as a class of objects? C++ is a case in point: it provides powerful object-oriented (OO) features, but programmers must define their own list classes. Sure, object libraries, such as NIHCL, provide such classes. But to use these, you must understand the behavior of list objects to apply them with confidence.

The objective of this chapter is show how lists can be modeled as *state machines*—not finite but "infinite" state machines, since lists need not have an upper bound on their lengths. This will help us to understand how to describe their behavior in the terms we have already introduced: namely, as responses to query-terminated sequences of commands.

The repertoire of list manipulations consists of a large number of queries and commands. Rather than try to characterize them all at once, it is more practical to start with a subset from which many others can be synthesized. Methods for building a bigger set of methods are called *primitives* for the bigger set.

We shall use the following primitives:

queries: length?, list-ref?

commands: insert, remove

The object behavior specification based on these primitives is shown in Figure 1.

list(element)

constructor

list make-list()

queries

number length?(list)
element list-ref?(list,number)

commands

list' insert(list,element,number)
list' remove(list,number)

Domain Restrictions

list-ref?(list,i) = defined provided that 0 <= i <= length?(list)-1
remove(list,i) = defined provided that 0 <= i <= length?(list)-1
insert(list,j) = defined provided that 0 <= j <= length?(list)

Equivalences

length?(make-list()) = 0
length?(insert(element,list,i)) = length?(list) + 1
length?(remove(element,list,i)) = length?(list) - 1

list-ref?(insert(element,list,i),i) = element
list-ref?(insert(element,list,i),j < i) = list-ref?(list,j)
list-ref?(insert(element,list,i),j > i) = list-ref?(list,j - 1)

list-ref?(remove(list,i), j < i) = list-ref?(list,j)
list-ref?(remove(list,i), j >= i) = list-ref?(list,j+1)

Figure 1. List object behavior specification.

3.1 Domain Restrictions and Legal Sequences

There is a slot in the specification form in Chapter 2 *called **Domain Restrictions***. This allows us to specify constraints on the combinations of argument values for any of the methods defined in the specification. For example, the only positions that have elements in a list are those between its boundaries, namely 0 and the length of the list minus 1. Thus in list-ref?(list,i) we must have $0 \leq i \leq$ length?(list) - 1 and we say that $0 \leq i \leq$ length?(list) - 1 is the domain restriction for list-ref?. Similar considerations apply to the domain restrictions on remove and insert.

Programmers often define exception conditions and implement exception handlers to deal with them. Such exception conditions are modeled as domain restrictions in object behavior specifications. For example, what should be the result of attempting to remove from an empty list? Although domain restrictions are an important part of behavior specification, we leave the decision of how to deal with domain violations (in other words, exception handling) up to the implementor. For example, two different implementations could both correctly implement the list class but differ in the way they treat the problem of removing from an empty list. One might prevent the removal from happening at all; another might return an empty list. By stating the domain restrictions, we define only the normal behavior of the object and expect it to be implemented correctly. This greatly simplifies the task of specification, since it leaves the abnormal behavior to the implementation, where the context of the implementation can be taken into account.

When domain restrictions are specified, not all query-terminated sequences are meaningful. We say that a sequence is *legal* if no domain restrictions are violated at any step within it. A sequence is *illegal* if at least one domain violation occurs. For example, the following is a **legal** sequence:

```
list' = make-list()
list'' = insert(element,list,0)
list-ref?(list'',0)
```

In contrast, following are **illegal** sequences:

```
list' = make-list()
list'' = insert(element,list,1)

list' = make-list()
list'' = insert(element,list,0)
list-ref?(list'',1)
```

Since the object behavior specification concerns itself only with capturing normal behavior it gives the desired responses associated with all the legal query-terminated sequences.

3.2 An Abstract Model for the List Specification

Figure 2 displays a list in abstract form divorced of any particular computer realization. This representation, or model, should help to understand how the object behavior specification for lists works. Intuitively, a list is, at any time, a finite sequence of elements—it can grow or contract, so its length may change. This suggests that the state of a list should be determined by its length and by its elements in the order they occur. The queries length? and list-ref? provide precisely this information. Let's state a criterion for a set of queries providing enough information to represent the state of an object—this has to be stated relative to a set of commands:

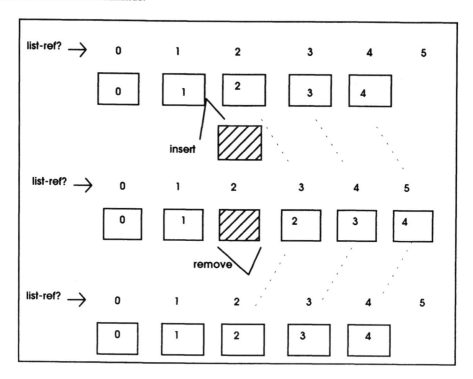

Figure 2. Lists in abstract form divorced of any computer realization.

A set of queries is a **state-representing set** if the value returned by each query, *after* any command, can be determined by knowing the values returned by the queries *before* the command was issued and the values of the arguments in the command.

By referring to Figure 2, you can see that length? and list-ref? are a state-representing set relative to insert and remove:

- The length of a list will increase (or decrease) by one whenever an element is inserted or removed. In other words, the value returned by length? is determined by its value before either command is issued. This is expressed by

length?(insert(element,list,i)) = length?(list) + 1
length?(remove(element,list,i)) = length?(list) + 1

- What happens to the value "read out" by list-ref? at various positions after inserting an element? Consider the *insertion point:* here list-ref? returns the element just inserted:

list-ref?(insert(element,list,i),i) = element

If the *read-out* point,j comes before the insertion point,i then the read-out shows no change.

list-ref?(insert(element,list,i), j < i) = list-ref?(list,j)

If the read-out point comes after the insertion point, then the element at the read-out point is what was read out by list-ref? at the preceding position before the insertion:

list-ref?(insert(element,list,i), j > i) = list-ref?(list, j - 1)

The reverse story happens in the case of remove:

list-ref?(remove(list,i), j < i) = list-ref?(list, j)
list-ref?(remove(list,i), j >= i) = list-ref?(list, j +1)

- To determine the list boundary we need to know its length. This explains why we need length? as a state representing query. The restrictions on insertion and read-out points are stated by the following:

0 <= i <= length?(list) - 1
0 <= j <= length?(list)

With one more piece of information—that the length of an empty list is zero—we can use the state equations just written to simulate the behavior of a list state machine. This provides us with a way of testing any particular implementation of a list class. The basic idea is that to be correct, an implementation must display the same behavior as that obtained in the simulation. We'll return to this idea later.

3.3 Implementations and Models of Lists

A very common way of implementing lists in such languages as Scheme or Lisp can be likened to a physical model consisting of two curtain rods with rings as elements. Figure 3 illustrates the correspondences underlying this analogy. The two rods hold the head and tail parts of the list. A read-out point can be anywhere on either rod. The insertion point (and removal point) is the gap between the rods. To insert a new element at a desired point, we have to move rings from one rod to the other across the gap until the desired insertion point lines up with the gap. The new ring is placed on the left-hand rod. To remove a ring, we get it into the end of the left rod and pull it off the gap.

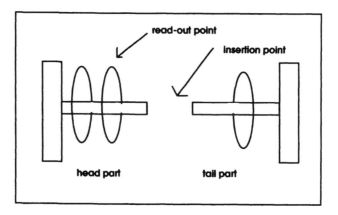

Figure 3. The curtain rod model of list implementation.

It is often helpful to visualize such physical models when constructing abstract data structures and other objects. Such *concrete representations* suggest ways to implement and test their computer counterparts. For example, the most common way to implement lists is through pointers, as we shall see in the later discussion of C++. Such implementations can be modeled by the *railway car* analogy illustrated in Figure 4.

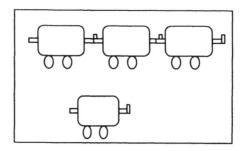

Figure 4. The railway car model of list implementation.

Here elements, the cars, are hooked together by coupling the hook of one into the ring of the next. To insert a new car between two linked cars, the two have to be uncoupled and the new car hooked into the car in front while having the car behind hook into it. A similar decoupling and recoupling is needed for removal. With toy cars that can be easily picked up, any such coupling can be easily modified. Not so for real railway cars confined to tracks! Here insertion, or removal, can only take place at a siding in a similar manner to the curtain rod model.

3.4 Parallel Implementations of Lists

So far we have considered only very standard computer implementations of lists along with their counterpart physical models. The memory of a conventional computer is organized as a (very long) sequence of words. There are only a few natural and efficient ways to implement sequential list structures in such a sequential memory. However, the rise of parallel computers may change all that. Parallel computers in the near future will have many thousands of processors, and it may be possible to implement lists in radically different ways—and get much faster execution as well. Imagine a "sea" of computers that can communicate with each other (Figure 5).

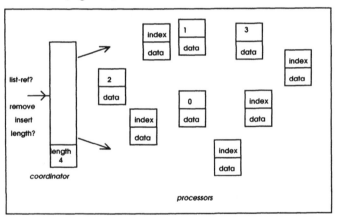

Figure 5. A massively parallel implementation of lists.

Two types of computers, coordinators and processors, cooperate to realize list-like behavior. Active processors store data and have an index representing their position in a list. A coordinator receives the external commands and queries. When it receives an insertion command, the coordinator recruits an inactive processor, giving it the proper index and data. The newly activated processor is "tuned" to listen to its current "boss." A remove command results in the deactivation of a processor, enabling it to return to the pool of inactive processors. The interaction between a coordinator and its listeners proceeds as follows (Figure 6).

Notice that in this "analogy," the sequential nature of a list is no longer reflected by a spatial arrangement as it was in previous models. Instead, each processor knows its position in the list and can easily and quickly update this information: it takes only two communication steps to complete each operation, no matter how long the list is! Later we will discuss how parallel implementations such as this can be neatly expressed in object-oriented terms.

```
when the coordinator receives list-ref?( i)
    If 0 <= i <= length - 1 }
        it broadcasts i to all processors simultaneously
        the processor whose index = i
            responds by returning its data.

when the coordinator receives insert?(x,i)
    If 0 <= i <= length
        it broadcasts i to all processors simultaneously
        the processors whose indexes >= i
            increment their indexes
        a new processor with index = i and data = x
            is activated to listen to this coordinator
                and length is incremented

when the coordinator receives remove( i)
    If 0 <= i <= length - 1
        it broadcasts i to all processors simultaneously
        concurrently:
        the processor whose index = i
            is deactivated and length is decremented
        the processors whose indexes >= i
            decrement their indexes
```

Figure 6. Parallel implementation of list behavior.

3.5 Proving and Testing Correctness

Several quite distinct implementations of list behavior have been discussed. Furthermore, many more are possible now or will become feasible in the future. So it should be clear that we urgently need means of establishing that an implementation is correct. Ideally, the required behavior should be stated in *abstract* terms *independently* of any implementation. Fortunately, the equations we developed for list behavior satisfy this criterion. Later we will see how such an approach allows us to formulate tests of behavior and sometimes prove that an implementation is correct.

Problems

1. Imagine a "rubber band" implementation of a list. In this model, every time an insertion needs to be done, the band is stretched uniformly to make room for the new entry. Write a class definition for lists such as that for the railway car model, where the rubber band is represented by a vector and stretching is represented by copying the vector into a new one twice its size. Discuss the obvious disadvantages of such an implementation with conventional computing technology. What might be its advantages in a technology for which stretching occurred without cost?

2. Write a suite of tests for class list that can be used to test the behavior of any implementation of this class. Show that your implementation in Problem 1 passes this suite of tests.

3. Simulate the behavior of a list object using the object behavior specification given in the text. That is, select several legal query-terminated sequences and work out the responses by following the step-by-step computation of successive states that we can do using the equations of the specification.

4. Append adds one list to the end of another so that they form one combined list. An elegant implementation of append is possible for the parallel "sea of processors" implementation provided that one coordinator can transfer its tuning frequency to another. Write a protocol, similar to those in the text, for appending one list to another.

5. (Optional: requires Scheme or Lisp background) Encapsulate lists, basic data structures in Scheme or Lisp, as a user-defined class, list. (Hint: define a single instance variable, lst, which will be treated as a (basic object) list. Define the methods list-ref? and remove to invoke the corresponding procedures of Scheme on lst. In many implementations, there is a small problem with this: using the name of a method within its definition will cause an infinite recursion. A simple but inelegant solution is to change the names of the methods. (There are more fundamental solutions but they are beyond the scope of this book.) Implement insert by using cons and cdr in curtain rod fashion. Discuss the differences between lists as basic data structures and lists as user-defined objects.

6. (Nonuniqueness of primitives). Show that the set {length?, head?,rest?, add-to-front, add-to-tail} is a set of primitives for list behavior, where

head?(list) = list-ref?(list,0)
insert(rest?(list), head?(list),0) = list
    //rest?(list) is list with the first element
    //removed (if any)
add-to-front(list, el) = insert(list,el,0)
add-to-tail(list, el) = insert(list,el,length?(list))

(Hint: show that each of the methods in the set {length?, list-ref?, insert, remove} can be expressed in terms of the given set—use the *curtain rod model* to do so.)

7. A *cursored list* has a cursor that moves one position at a time between the boundaries. The public commands are move_left, move_right, insert and re-move at the cursor position. The public queries are at_left_end?, at_right-_end?, and read? at the cursor position. Write an object behavior specification for the class cursored list. (Hint: retain the queries of list as hidden and add a hid-den query, cursor_position?. Write the state equations for all pairs of state-representing queries and constructor/commands.)

4
Inheritance Hierarchies and Hierarchical Construction

This chapter introduces the concept of *inheritance* in object-oriented programming and design. Inheritance is an essential and powerful mechanism that enables new classes to be constructed on the basis of existing classes. Inheritance also helps to organize large software systems into manageable pieces through *inheritance hierarchies*. We also discuss a related concept, *hierarchical construction*, often called *aggregation* in database contexts, that allows software modules to be connected together to form larger systems.

We will start by taking on the task of developing a class of objects that can realize any desired switching function. For example, Figure 1 shows a switching function called and-gate. It has two input wires which can take on binary values, often represented by 0 and 1, or by FALSE and TRUE. The response of the and-gate to each combination of its inputs is shown in the table. A concise description of this behavior is that its output is the logical conjunction of its inputs (i.e., output = input1 and input2). In other words, both inputs must be TRUE for the output to be TRUE.

The and-gate is an example of a switching function. Other examples are the two input or-gate and the one input not-gate also shown in Figure 1. There are an infinite number of others, each having a finite number of inputs and one output. It is well known that the and, or, and not gates form a set of **primitives** for all switching functions in the sense that any function can be built by interconnecting copies of these primitives. Thus, there are at least two ways of implementing a particular switching function: (1) directly, and (2) as a network of primitives.

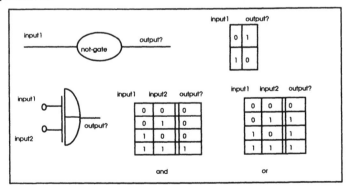

Figure 1. Logic gates.

In this chapter we will show how the mechanism of inheritance greatly facilitates defining classes of objects such as switching functions that can be synthesized both directly and through network synthesis using hierarchical construction.

4.1 Specifying and Implementing an and-gate

The background for our inheritance presentation is set by considering how the and-gate might be implemented as an object. We assume that inputs arrive one at a time. Therefore, Figure 2 shows that there are two commands for inserting input1 and input2, respectively. Reset is a third command to prepare for another round. Output? is a query to obtain the and-gate response to its last two inputs. Ready? tells if both inputs have been received since the last reset.

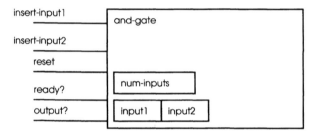

Figure 2. Interface for and-gate.

The object behavior specification for the and-gate is shown in Figure 3. To obtain a state-representing set of queries, we add the queries num-inputs? (the number received so-far), input1? (the last received value of input1), and input2? (ditto for input2). Ready? can be defined directly in terms of num-inputs?, and output? is defined directly in terms of the inputs. Therefore, neither needs to be included in the basic queries. Since there are 3 queries and 3 commands plus a constructor, there are 12 (= 3 x 4) cases defined in the specification.

A class declaration for and-gate in C++ is shown in Figure 4. We start by making some declarations that help the readability of C++ code.

    enum { FALSE,TRUE };

defines FALSE to mean 0 and TRUE to mean 1

    typedef unsigned int boolean;

defines boolean to a new type having the same properties as unsigned int — C++ terminology for non-negative integers. (When possible, we save space by using unsigned int instead of int, which includes the sign.)

and-gate

constructor
and-gate make-and-gate()

queries

Derived
bool output?(and-gate)
bool ready?(and-gate)

hidden
bool input1?(and-gate)
bool input2?(and-gate)
num num-inputs?(and-gate)

commands
and-gate' insert-input1(and-gate,bool)
and-gate' insert-input2(and-gate,bool)
and-gate' reset(and-gate)

Equivalences
input1?(make-and-gate()) = F
input2?(make-and-gate()) = F
num-inputs?(make-and-gate()) = 0
input1?(insert-input1(and-gate,bool))= bool
input2?(insert-input1(and-gate,bool)) = input2?(and-gate)
        //the value in input2 does not depend on the input1
num-inputs?(insert-input1(and-gate,bool)) = num-inputs?(and-gate) + 1
input1?(insert-input2(and-gate,bool))= input1?(and-gate)
        //the value in input1 does not depend on the input2
input2?(insert-input2(and-gate,bool)) = bool
num-inputs?(insert-input2(and-gate,bool)) = num-inputs?(and-gate) + 1
num-inputs?(reset(and-gate)) = 0
                //reset doesn't clear the stored inuts just the count
                //of received values

Domain Restrictions
output?(and-gate) = defined if ready?(and-gate) = T

Definitions
ready?(and-gate) = (num-inputs?(and-gate) = 2)
output?(and-gate) = and(input1?(and-gate),input2?(and-gate))

Figure 3. and-gate object behavior specification.

```
class and_gate{

private:
boolean input1;
boolean input2;
int num_inputs;

public:

and_gate(){
reset();
}


void insert_input1(boolean inp){
input1 = inp;
num_inputs++;
}

void insert_input2(boolean inp){
input2 = inp;
num_inputs++;
}

 void reset(){
  num_inputs = 0;
 }

boolean ready_q(){
return num_inputs == 2;
}

boolean output(){
return input1 && input2;
}
};
```

Figure 4. C++ class declaration for and-gate.

Examples of query-terminated sequences for the and-gate include:

```
and_gate a = new and_gate;
a->ready(); --> FALSE
a-> insert-input1TRUE);
a-> insert-input2 TRUE);
```

```
a->ready(); -->TRUE
a->output(); -->TRUE

a->reset();
a->ready(); --> FALSE
a-> insert-input1TRUE);
a-> insert-input2 FALSE);
a->ready(); -->TRUE
a->output(); -->FALSE
```

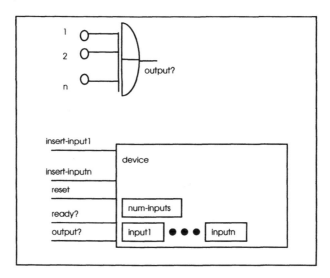

Figure 5. The General switching function.

4.2 General Switching Functions

Figure 5 illustrates the general switching function that has n inputs and one output. We can try to formulate the behavior specification for a class of devices that can implement these switching functions as shown in Figure 6. Actually, since there is no limit on the number of possible input wires for such a function, the specification is given in *parameterized* form. The number of input wires, n, and the switching function, fn, are assumed to be *parameters*. For example, the and-gate is obtained by putting n = 2 and fn = and.

```
device (n,fn)

constructor

device make-device()

queries

hidden

bool input1?(device)
...
bool inputn?(device)
num num-inputs?(device)

commands

device' insert-input1(device,bool)
...
device' insert-inputn(device,bool)
device' reset(device)


Equivalences


input1?(make-device()) = F
...
inputn?(make-device()) = F
num-inputs?(make-device()) = 0


input1?(insert-input1(device,bool ))= bool
...
inputn?(insert-input1(device,bool)) = inputn?(device)
...
input1?(insert-inputn(device,bool )) =  input1?(device)
...
inputn?(insert-inputn(device,bool)) = bool

num-inputs?(insert-input1(device,bool)) = num-inputs?(device) + 1

 input1?(reset(device)) = input1?(device)
...
 inputn?(reset(device)) = inputn?(device)
 num-inputs?(reset(device)) = 0

Derived

 bool output?(device)
 bool ready?(device)

Domain Restrictions
 output?(device) = defined if ready?(device) = T

Definitions

 ready?(device) = (num-inputs?(device ) = n)
 output?(device) = fn(input1?(device),...,inputn?(device))
```

Figure 6. Object behavior specification for devices (switching functions).

4.3 Inheritance and Derived Classes in C++

Figure 7 depicts the inheritance hierarchy for class device and its subclasses. Our C++ implementation of this hierarchy uses instance variables to implement hidden methods. In general, we distinguish between a *behavior inheritance hierarchy* that specifies the behavior of a collection of classes from an *implementation inheritance* hierarchy that represents the way this collection of classes is implemented in a particular language or environment. The distinction between behavior and implementation is as important in the context of a collection of classes as it is when dealing with one class. For example, we will see later that the container hierarchy is best specified with one hierarchical structure but that different hierarchical structures are better suited for serial as opposed to parallel implementation.

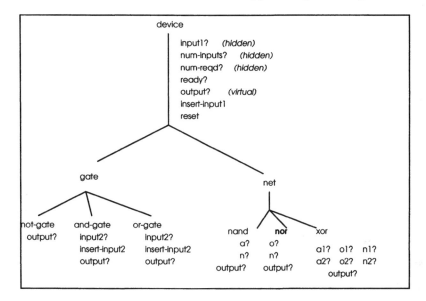

Figure 7. Behavior hierarchy for device and its derived classes.

The interface declaration for device is shown in Figure 8. One major new feature to notice is that we have used the access qualifier protected in place of private. This is because we are looking ahead to using device as a base class to derive other classes using inheritance} in C++. For example, gate and net will be derived from device. C++ stipulates that private members of a base class are accessible only in the scope of the base class, not in those of its derived classes. Thus, as shown in Figure 9, private members of a base class are not accessible to the methods of any derived class. Now we want the instance variables that are *private* in *device* also to be private (and accessible) in a derived class such as and_gate. Thus, we designate these as protected — in accordance with the access inheritance rules in Figure 9, which summarizes the rules for all combinations of allowed access combinations of base and derived classes.

Another feature to notice in Figure 8 is the use of virtual in the declaration of the output method. We said earlier that this indicates that each derived class is expected to supply its own version of output. However, in C++, the real role of virtual is to support the important mechanism of dynamic binding — to which we will return later.

```
class device {

protected: //indicates that the following variables are private
        //and moreover, when inherited they are protected
        //(hence also private)
        //in any derived class

boolean input1;
unsigned int num_inputs;
unsigned int num_reqd;


public: // indicates that the following methods are in the
        // public interface
device();
boolean ready();
virtual boolean output(); // tells the compiler that derived
                // classes will provide their
                //own version of this method
void insert_input1(boolean in);
void reset();

};


device::device()
{
num_reqd = 1;
}
```

Figure 8. Class interface declaration for device

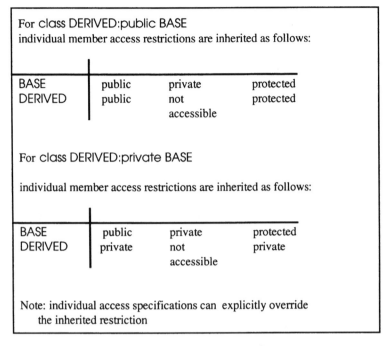

For class DERIVED:public BASE
individual member access restrictions are inherited as follows:

BASE	public	private	protected
DERIVED	public	not accessible	protected

For class DERIVED:private BASE

individual member access restrictions are inherited as follows:

BASE	public	private	protected
DERIVED	private	not accessible	private

Note: individual access specifications can explicitly override
   the inherited restriction

Figure 9. Access inheritance in C++.

    Figure 10 shows classes gate and net declared as derived classes of device. Since the qualifier public is used, the rules in Figure 9 say that gate and net will each inherit all the public and protected members of device and treat them as public and protected, respectively. Most often we use the public modifier in deriving a class. However, we can use private instead. As shown in Figure 9, the effect of this is to make the public members of the base class private in the derived class. There are occasions when this makes perfect sense—when we want to totally encapsulate the base class so that only the derived interface is exposed (see the Problems). Now look at the constructors for gate and net in Figure 10. In C++, base class constructors are not inherited. However, they can be invoked within derived class constructors to have the same constructive effect. For example, since gate is derived from device, we can call the device constructor to perform a suitable initialization of num-read. Of course, within its body, the derived class constructor can still perform any other initializations that are relevant to the derived class.

```
class gate:public device // declares gate to be a class derived
            // from base class device
{
gate():device(){}
};

class net:public device
{
net():device(){}
};
```

Figure 10. Deriving gate and net from device.

```
class not_gate:public gate
{
public:
not_gate();
boolean output(); // indicates that not_gate is
            // providing its own version
};
```

Figure 11. Deriving not_gate from gate.

```
class and_gate:public gate
{
private:
boolean input2;
public:
and_gate();
void insert_input2(boolean in);
boolean output(); // indicates that and_gate is
            // providing its own version
}

and_gate::and_gate()
{
num_reqd = 2;
}
```

Figure 12. Deriving and_gate from gate.

Figures 11 and 12 depict the derivation of not_gate and and_gate from gate, respectively. Notice that the methods ready, insert_input1, and reset are inherited without change from device (see the Problems).

4.4 Using Inheritance for Alternative Implementations

While every switching function can be implemented with the approach embodied in class gate, this approach may not be the most convenient, or even feasible, when the number of inputs gets to be large. Indeed, hardware designers must contend with such extremely large switching functions. Therefore, we provide an alternative approach embodied in a new subclass called net. Its definition simply declares it to be a subclass of device and enables it to inherit all the features defined for this class:

    net: inherit from device

The new approach in net is to construct a switching function by synthesizing its behavior from a network of components. These components must have already been defined as classes of device. Initially, they may be subclasses of gate—and indeed, the primitives and_gate, or_gate, and not_gate are sufficient for this purpose. However, once a new subclass has been defined, it can be **reused** as a component to make an even larger network. Thus *hierarchical construction* is possible.

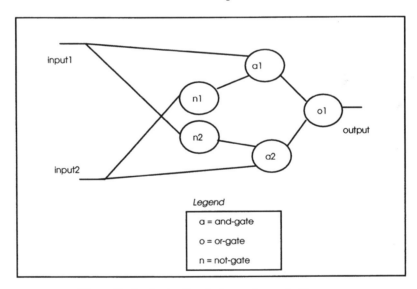

Figure 13. Synthesis of exclusive-or from primitives.

Figure 13 depicts a network synthesis of the exclusive-or switching function. This function outputs a 1 just in case its inputs are different – it is like an or except that it excludes the case where both inputs are 1s.

The implementation of the exclusive-or network as class xor is shown in Figure 14. In the class definition we have an instance variable for each component in the network. For example, we have instance variables a1 and n1 holding pointers to an and_gate and a not_gate, respectively. In C++, pointers must be *declared* as data members in a class declaration. They must be *defined* (i.e., given an appropriate instance to point to in the class methods), usually in a constructor. For example, the pointers, a1 and n1, are given the addresses of and_gate and not_gate instances, respectively, in the constructor xor_gate().

The method output() propagates the input values to the components in the proper sequence—making sure that a component receives all its inputs before sending its output to the next level. When the highest-level component has finally received all its inputs, its output is generated to be the output of the net.

The following query-terminated sequence tests the behavior of an xor instance. It also illustrates the use of the features inherited from device.

```
int main()

{
xor * x = new xor();  // declare and define instance of xor
x->insert_input1(FALSE);  // inherited from device
x->insert_input2(TRUE);
if (x->ready())        // inherited from device
{
if (x->output() ==FALSE)
cout << "test satisfied:";
else  cout << "test not satisfied:";
}
x->reset();          // inherited from device
... // start next test
}
```

```
class xor:public net{
private:
boolean input2;
and_gate * a1; // declare instance variable to be a
              // pointer to type and_gate
and_gate * a2;
not_gate * n1;
not_gate * n2;
or_gate * o1;


public:
xor();
void insert_input2(boolean in);
boolean output();
}

xor::xor()
{
num_reqd = 2;
a1 = new and_gate();// define value of instance variable
              // to be instance of and_gate
a2 = new and_gate();
n1 = new not_gate();
n2 = new not_gate();
o1 = new or_gate();
 }

void xor::insert-input2(boolean inp){
  input2  = inp;
  num_inputs++;
}


xor::output()
{
n1->insert_input1(input2);
n2->insert_input1(input1);
a1->insert_input1(input1);
a1->insert_input2(n1->output());
a2->insert_input2(input2);
a2->insert_input1(n2->output());
o1->insert_input1(a1->output());
o1->insert_inpu21(a2->output());
return o1->output();:
 }
```

Figure 14. Class xor derived from class net in C++.

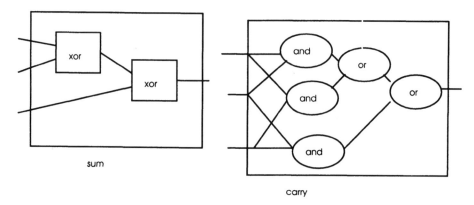

sum

carry

Figure 15. Sum and carry components of binary adder.

4.5 Hierarchical Construction

As mentioned before, predefined classes can be employed to provide components for larger nets. Figure 15 shows an example where two xor instances are connected together to implement a device called sum. The class definition is simple (Figure 16).

```
class sum: public net{
private:
boolean input2;
boolean input3;
xor * x1;
xor * x2;

public:
sum();
void insert_input2(boolean in);
void insert_input3(boolean in);
boolean output();
};
```

Figure 16. Class definition for sum.

The definition of the class methods is an exercise at the end of the chapter. The sum switching function does a very useful job when considered as operating on 0s and 1s. Indeed, it is part of the addition hardware in a digital computer. When two binary words are added, each pair of bits is added together using modulo 2 addition (xor) and the result is added to the bit carried from the previous pair. The carry bit is also a switching function that yields a 1 just in case there are at least 2 ones in the input. An implementation of the carry function is also shown in Figure 15; its class definition is left as an exercise.

The construction of a binary adder illustrates the power of **hierarchical construction**. In such *bottom-up* construction, the final device is synthesized in stages where components at the next stage are built from components at the current or earlier stages. Each stage involves one or more classes that can be tested and debugged before their use in subsequent stages.

4.6 Summary

Inheritance is the replication of features, such as instance variables and methods, already defined for one class to the definition of another. Designating a *superclass* in a class declaration lets this class inherit all the features of the designated superclass. The new class is now called a *subclass*, or *derived class*, of the latter superclass, or *base class*.

- Inherited features may be used without modification in a subclass, or they may be overridden by local definitions as needed. New features may also be added that make use of inherited ones.
- Inheritance is the basic organizing concept in class hierarchies that provide alternative means to construct objects that have many commonalities, but also significant differences.
- Hierarchical construction is performed by reusing instances of already defined classes as components in larger networks.

Problems

1. Specify the behavior of the subclasses of net: nor (which is not applied to the result of or) and nand (which is not applied to and).
2. Specify the behavior of subclasses of net to implement the following 3 input switching functions:
    a) outputs a TRUE just in case all its inputs are TRUE
    b) outputs a TRUE just in case at least one of its inputs is TRUE
    c) outputs a TRUE just in case at least one of its inputs is FALSE
    (Hint: equivalently, it outputs a TRUE just in case not all its inputs are TRUE.)
3. Supply the missing definitions for methods ready, insert-input1, and reset in the class definition of device (Figure 8). Remember that they must be inherited without change, for example, in the definition of and_gate. (Hint: in ready use num-reqd, which is initialized upon instantiation).
4. Complete the C++ implementation of the device hierarchy (Figure 1). Implement and test the xor derived class.
5. Define the method output for the subclasses sum and carry, respectively, in Figure 15.
6. (a) Extend the use of class net to allow for more than one output. For example, connect a sum instance and a carry instance to form a three-input, two-output half-adder. Continuing with hierarchical construction, n of these half-adders can

be connected together to form a full adder for n-bit binary numbers. Define such a class for n = 4.

(b) Implement and test the four-bit binary full-adder in C++.

7. Notice that the object behavior specification for device given in the text assumes that inputs are not repeated between resets, e.g., insert-input1 does not occur twice, causing and-gate to consider itself ready for output when actually only one of the input wires has been activated. Revise the behavior specification to declare any duplicated input between resets to be illegal. Revise the C++ implementation. How does this change what can be inherited?

8. Rewrite the specification of cursored_list (Problem 7, Chapter 3) by inheriting the specification of class list and writing only those new query/command pairs that are not specified in list.

5

Containers: An Object Behavior Specification

Chapter 3 presented an object behavior specification of the list class and explained the advantages of such a specification. We saw that there are many ways to implement list behaviors – in particular, sequential and parallel implementations differ radically. In Chapter 1 we mentioned that containers are basic classes that help store, retrieve and organize interacting objects. We said then that containers were generalized forms of lists. Actually, once we have freed ourselves from thinking in sequential processing terms, we can start with container as the more basic concept and derive lists as one of the special subclasses that happen to be natural for sequential processing but are not really fundamental in general.

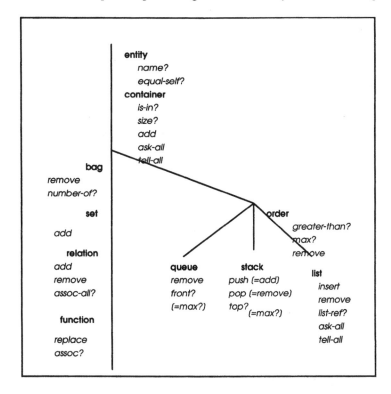

Figure 1. Behavior class hierarchy for container.

This chapter introduces the specification hierarchy of the container classes shown in Figure 1. The classes are roughly characterized as follows:

- container – the base class, provides basic services for the derived classes;
- bag – counts multiple object occurrences;
- set – only one occurrence of any object is allowed;
- relation – is a set of key-value pairs, used in dictionary fashion;
- function – is a relation in which only one occurrence of any key allowed;
- order – maintains items in given order;
- queue – maintains items in first-in/first-out (FIFO) order;
- stack – maintains items in last-in/first-out (LIFO) order;
- list – maintains items in order determined by an insertion index.

This chapter presents the unordered container lineage of the container hierarchy: bag –> set –> relation –> function. Chapter 10 will continue with ordered classes. We will also introduce the concept of *ensemble methods*, which are related to the more common concept of class iterators, but are equally at home in both serial and parallel implementations. In a later chapter, we will discuss an implementation in C++ that can hide the underlying hardware so that both serial and parallel/distributed environments can be accommodated.

5.1 Class entity

As shown in Figure 1, container is actually a subclass of the more basic class, entity. This latter class will actually be the base class for all user-defined classes whose instances can be placed into container instances. Class entity will provide methods that work hand-in-glove with those of container. Note that since container is derived from entity, container instances can be placed into other container instances, thus setting up the basis for hierarchical construction.

The object behavior specification for entity is given in Figure 2.

---

entity

constructor

entity make-entity(name)

queries

name name?(entity)
entity equal-self?(entity,entity1)

commands

equivalences

name?(make-entity(name)) = name

equal-self?(entity,entity) = entity

equal-self?(entity,entity1) = make-entity("null")

Figure 2. entity behavior specification.

As you see, entity has only two queries, but these are essential for later use. One provides the object's printable name. The other provides a test of equality: an instance is able to recognize whether any other instance is its equal; in such a case, the instance itself is returned. This will be very convenient soon when we scan containers for instances that match given requirements. When appropriate, the method says roughly: "I match your requirements and here I am." We will add more methods to entity as we need them.

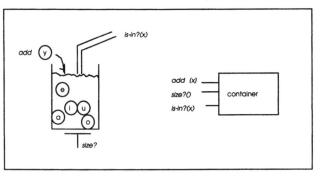

Figure 3. The basic methods of container.

5.2 Container Base Class

We are ready to specify the behavior of the container base class. As shown in
Figure 3, it has only the most basic functionality. We can

- add instances of entity (but not yet remove them),
- ask how many items there are, and
- ask whether a specific object is included in the container.

We have purposely chosen is-in? and size? to form a state-representing set of queries.
Writing the specification then becomes straightforward (Figure 4).

```
container(entity) inherited from entity

constructor

container make-container()

queries

number size?(container)
boolean  is-in? (container,entity)

commands

container' add(container,entity)

Equivalences

size?(make-container()) =0
size?(add(container,entity)) = size?(container) + 1

is-in?(make-container()entity) =F
is-in?(add(container,entity),entity)) = T
is-in?(add(container,entity),entity1)) =
                                is-in?(container,entity 1)
      //the state of container relative to
      //entity1 is not affected by the
      //addition of a different entity
```

Figure 4. Basic container specification.

To illustrate how containers can be used, let us create two containers of vowels and consonants, respectively (Figure 5):

```
vowels = make-container()
consonants=make-container()
size? (vowels) = 0
a = make-entity("a")
...;; make all letters
z = make-entity("z")

vowels' = add(vowels,a)
...;; add all vowels

vowels⁶ = add(vowels⁵,y)

consonants' = add(consonants,b)
...;; add all consonants

consonants²⁶ = add(consonants,z)
```

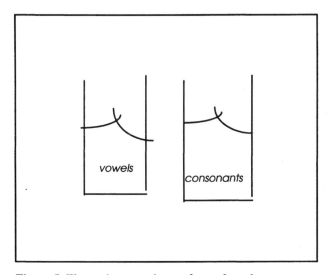

Figure 5. Illustrating containers of vowels and consonants.

Tests of whether a letter is a vowel, consonant, or both (as in the letter y) use the method is-in? as follows:

is-in?(vowels, a) = T
is-in?(vowels, b) = F
is -in?(vowels, y) = T
is-in?(consonants, y)= T
size?(vowels) = 6
size?(consonants) = 21

Now suppose that we want to test whether a letter is a vowel or a consonant in one step. For this we need to add both vowel and consonant containers to another container. To check whether a letter is a vowel, a consonant, or both, we query the individual containers simultaneously using is-in?. The ensemble methods, discussed next, provide the right vehicles for such tasks.

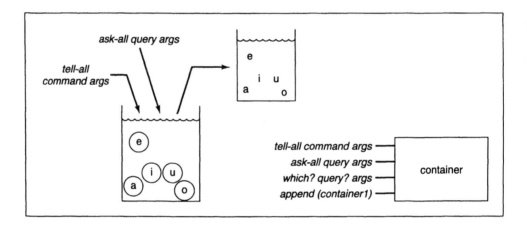

Figure 6. Class container ensemble methods.

5.3 Ensemble Methods

Figure 6 illustrates the basic methods that allow us to treat all the items in a container as a group. We call these *ensemble methods* since they apply to the ensemble, or whole, container at once. There is one primitive command, tell-all, which is *primitive* in the sense that others can be synthesized from it (not in the sense of being simple, since it depends on a good deal of capability in the underlying environment). The behavior of the ensemble methods is informally described by

- tell-all(container,command,args)–sends *command(args)* to each entity in the container;
- ask-all(container,query?,args) – sends *query?(args)* to each entity in the container and collects the results in a container;

- which?(container,query?,args)—sends *query?(args)* to each entity in the container and collects the entities which return T in a container;
- append(container,container1)—adds the entities in container 1 to those in container.

The object behavior specification for the above ensemble methods is given in terms of the effects of queries and commands on the state-representing queries in Figure 7.

Examples

Here are some examples of ensemble command use. Using tell-all, we can print out the vowels and consonants:

tell-all(vowels,display-name) // prints aeiouy

tell-all(consonants,display-name) //prints bcdfghjklmnpqrstvwxyz

The container created by ask-all is illustrated by

as = ask-all(vowels,equal-name,"a")

It has five null entities and the entity a. On the other hand, the container created by:

wa = which?(vowels,equal-name?,"a")

is a container whose only item is the entity a. Thus,

size?(wa) = 1

As in Figure 8, we can combine vowels and consonants into one container using append:

letters = make-container()

letters' = append(letters,vowels)

letter' = append(letters',consonants)

size?(letters'') = 27 // y is in twice

Ensemble Methods

---

command

container' tell-all(container,command,args)
        //results in changed states of all objects in container
container' append(container,container1)
            //adds in container1 contents to container

query

container1 ask-all(container,query?,args) //returns a container of answers
container1 which?(container,query?,args) //returns a container of entities
                            // which return T to query

Domain Restrictions

tell-all(container,command,args) = defined provided that
        if is-in?(entity,container) = T then command(entity,args) is defined

ask-all(container,query?,args) = defined provided that
        if is-in?(entity,container) = T then query?(entity,args) is defined

which?(container,query?,args) = defined provided that
        if is-in?(entity,container) = T then query?(entity,args) returns a boolean

Equivalences

is-in?(container,entity) = T   =>
        is-in?(tell-all(container,query?,args),command(entity,args)) = T
size?(tell-all(container,query?,args)) = size?(container)

is-in?(container,entity1) = T and query?(entity1, args) = entity
            => is-in?(ask-all(container,query?,args), entity) = T

size?(ask-all(container,query?,args)) = size?(container)

is-in?(container,entity) = T and query?(entity, args) = T
                <=> is-in?(which?(container,query?,args), entity) = T

size?(which?(container,query?,args)) <= size?(container)

is-in?(append(container,container1),entity) ==(is-in?(container,entity)= T or

                                        is-in?(container1,entity) = T)
size?(append(container,container1)) = size?(container) + size?(container1)

Figure 7. Container ensemble methods specification.

In contrast, we can add the two containers, vowels and consonants, as distinct items to a new container to form a partition[1] of the alphabet

```
partition  = make(container)
partition' = add(partition,vowels)
partition" = add(partition',consonants)
```

partition is an example of **hierarchical construction**: its entities are containers themselves. To find out, in one step, to which container(s) a letter belongs, we use the ensemble method, which?.

```
size?(which?(partition,is-in?,a) =1
```

```
size?(which? (partition, is-in?, y)) = 2
```

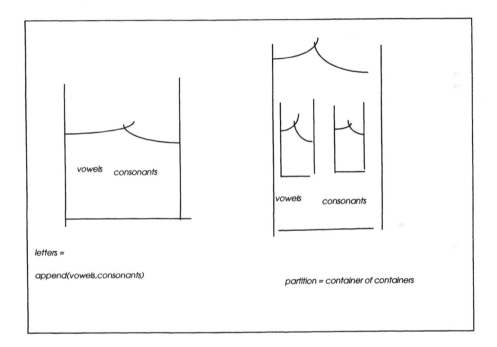

Figure 8. Appending versus partitioning.

We will continue exploring ensemble methods in Chapter 9.

---

[1] Mathematically speaking, this is a *cover* rather than a *partition*, since y is common to both blocks. However, we use the term "partition" since it is more suggestive and more easily understood to the less mathematically astute.

5.4 Container Subclasses: Unordered

This section deals with the unordered container lineage of the container hierarchy: bag → set → relation → function. We will continue with the ordered container classes in a later chapter. We take advantage of inheritance to specify each of the four subclasses. That is, we assume that all specifications of the base class apply to the derived class. For the latter, we have to provide only the new specifications not applicable in the base class and any inherited specifications in need of modification.

Bags and Sets

Sets are the fundamental building blocks of modern mathematics. A set is an unordered collection in which no element occurs more than once. Set theory goes back to the beginning of the 20th century. *Bags* are a more recent generalization of sets that allow any number of occurrences of elements. Mathematically speaking, it would make sense to start with set as the root class in a hierarchy for container. However, our objective is not mathematical, but computational, and this drives our choice of a root class that is even more generalized than bags. As shown in Figure 1, our root class has the bare minimum of methods that will be common to all containers. This simple core enables us to derive sets and other traditional mathematical containers from the base class. Ordered classes such as lists, stacks, and queues are also derived from the base class. We proceed to discuss the container hierarchy starting with classes bag and set.

Class bag, specified in Figure 9 adds the capability to query for the number of occurrences of an entity. It also introduces a remove command. The number of occurrences of each element is a state-representing query, and the effect of the commands add (inherited from the base class) and remove is easily characterized in terms of it. **Note that the specification of a derived class has to deal only with the new combinations of queries and commands that were not covered in the specification of the base class.**

Bag

bag(entity) inherits from *container*

constructor

bag make-bag()

queries

number number-of? (bag,entity)

commands

bag' remove(bag,entity)

Domain Restrictions

remove(bag,entity) = defined provided that is-in?(bag,entity) = T

Equivalences   //beyond those inherited from the parent in the hierarchy

size?(remove(bag,entity)) = size?(bag) - 1
                    // other combinations are inherited

number-of?(make-bag(),entity) = 0

number-of?(add(bag,entity),entity)) = number-of?(bag,entity) + 1
number-of?(add(bag,entity),entity 1)) = number-of?(bag,entity 1)

number-of?(remove(bag,entity),entity)) = number-of?(bag,entity) -1
          //remove acts to remove an instance of an entity

number-of(remove(bag,entity),entity 1)) = number-of(bag,entity 1)

Figure 9. Class bag specification.

Using a bag is appropriate where counts of element occurrences need to be maintained:

bg = make-bag
bg' = add(bg,a)

bg'' = add(bg',b)

bg''' = add(bg'',a)

number-of?(bg''',a) = 2

number-of?(bg''',b) = 1

number-of?(bg''',c) = 0

bg^{iv} = remove(bg''',a)

number-of(bg^{iv},a) = 1

Class set

The hierarchy shown in Figure 1 considers class set as a derived class of bag. As indicated before, sets, as mathematical objects, contain at most one occurrence of any entity. We specify this behavior by modifying the specification of add: we don't allow add to have an effect if the object to be added is already in the container. This is an example of a specification in a subclass overriding the specification inherited from the parent class. In the specification in , the size of a set increases only when a new entity is added:

---

set(entity) inherits from *bag*

constructor

set make-set()

queries

commands

set' add(set,entity)

Equivalences

All equivalences inherited from *bag* apply except for the effect
of add on size? And number-of? Which are specified by:

is-in?(set,entity) = F => seize?(add(set,entity)) + size(set) + 1
size?(add(set,entity)) = size?(set)   //otherwise

number-of?(add(set,entity),entity)) = 1
                              //increases to, and stays at, 1

number-of?(add(set,entity),entity1)) = number-of?(set,entity1)

Figure 10. Class set specification.

Set objects are used when keeping track of the very existence of an entity is important –
not how many times it has occurred. For example:

```
s = make-set()
s' = add(s,a);
s'' = add(s',a);
size?(s''') = 1
number-of? (s'',a) = 1
is-in?(s'',a) = T
s''' = remove(s'',a);
is-in?(s''',a) = F
```

Class Relation

Mathematically, a *binary relation* is a set of pairs. Likewise, we specify the class relation to inherit from set. The elements of such a set are called (key, value) pairs. Thus, the queries of relation have the form:

```
number size?(relation)
boolean is-in?(relation,key,value)
```

and the commands take the form:

```
relation' add(relation,key,value)
relation' remove(relation value),key,
```

The new behavior obtainable from class relation is to be able to retrieve all the values associated with a given key. This functionality is implemented in the query assoc-all?. We may also ask whether a key has already been given a value using key_is_in?. The specification follows (Figure 11):

Relations are used to record and lookup various kinds of associated data. For example, a dictionary associates words with meanings – the same word may have multiple meanings and different words may have the same meanings, as in:

```
r = make-relations()
key-is-in?(r,bit) = F
r' = add(r,bit,unit-of-information)
key-is-in(r',bit) = T
is-in?(r',bit,unit-of-information) = T
r'' = add(r',bit,small)
assoc-all?(r'',bit) = instance of set containing {unit-of-information,small}

r''' = add(r'',tiny,small)

assoc-all?(r''',bit) = instance of set containing {unit-of-information,small}
```

---

relation(entity) inherit from *set*

constructor

relation make-relation()

queries

number size?(relation)   //inherited from *set* (see text)
number number-of?(relation,key,value)
boolean is-in?(relation,key,value)

boolean key-is-in?(relation,key)
set assoc-all?(relation,key)   //returns a set of values

commands

relation' add(relation,key,value)
relation' remove(relation,key,value)

Domain Restrictions:

remove(relation,key,value) = defined provided that
                                      is-in?(relation,key,value) = T

Equivalences

We obtain the equivalences of relation by replacing
entity by key,value everywhere in the
equivalences inherited from sets. For example,

size?(add(relation,key,value)) = size?(relation) + 1.

Additional equivalences:

assoc-all?(make-relation(),key) = make-set()
assoc-all?(add(relation,key,value),key =
                          add(assoc-all?(relation,key),value)
assoc-all?(add(relation,key,value)key1) = assoc-all?(relation,key1)
assoc-all?(remove(relation,key,value),key) =
                          remove(assoc-all?(relation,key),vlaue)
assoc-all?(remove(relation,key,value),key1) = assoc-all?(relation,key1)
key-is-in?(relation,key) == (not(empty?(assoc-all?(relation,key))))

Figure 11. Class relation specification.

Class Function

A *function* is a relation for which at most one value is associated with any key (Figure 12). In the specification of class function we hide the command add inherited from relation. In its stead, there is a new command, replace, to enforce the "unique key" constraint on key-value pairs. However, method add can be used within the implementation of replace

Table-look up is a common form of function usage. For example, you can look up a table for the logarithm of a number (or approximate the logarithm using numbers in the table that are close to the given number). For example,

```
f = make-function()
key-is-in?(f, 5)     = F
f' = replace(f, 5, 6983)              //    put in approximation to log 5
assoc? (f', 5) = .6983                //    look-up log 5
key-is-in? (f', 5) = T
f'' = replace (f', 5.1 .7075)
assoc? (f'', 5.1) = .7075
f''' = replace(f'', 5.1, .7076)
                         //    put in better approximation to log 5.1

assoc? (f''', 5.1) = .7076
```

function(entity) inherit from *relation*

constructor

function make-function()

queries

value assoc?(function,key)

commands

function replace(function,key,value)

hidden

function add(function,key,value)

Domain Restrictions

assoc?(function,key) = defined provided
                        that is-in?(function,key) = F

Equivalences

is-in?(replace(function,key,value),key,value) = T
is-in?(replace(function,key,value),key,value1) = F

is-in?(replace(function,key1,value1),key,value)
                          = is-in?(function,key,value)

key-is-in?(function,key) = F => size?(replace(function,
                      key,value)) = size(function) + 1

size?(replace(function,key,value)) = size?(function)

assoc?(replace(function,key,value),key) = value

assoc?(replace(function,key,value),key1) =
                         assoc?(function,key1)

Note: assoc?(remove(function,key),key) = undefined

Figure 12. Class function specification.

Problems

1. Define a method to test whether a container is empty by:

    boolean empty?(container)

    empty?(container) == (size?(container) = 0)

    Use the specification of container to show that *empty?* satisfies the specification:

    empty?(make-container()) = T
    empty?(add(container,entity)) = F

2. Show that the following equivalences for ask-all and tell-all, respectively, satisfy the equations given for them in the container specification:

    ask-all (make-container(),query?,args)
          = make-container()
    ask-all(add(container,entity), query?,args)
        = add(ask-all(container,query?,args),
            query?(entity,args))

    tell-all (make-container(),command,args)
      = make-container()
    tell-all(add(container,entity),command,args)
        = add(tell-all(container,
          command, args), command(entity,args))

3. Show how to define ensemble methods ask-all and which? in terms of tell-all (Hint: introduce a command method for entity that deposits the result of a query into a given container.)

6
C++ Implementation of a Heterogeneous Container Class Library

This chapter discusses an implementation of the containers hierarchy in C++ called *Heterogeneous Container Class Library* (HCCL). Recall that "container" refers to a list-like structure to store data items, and "heterogeneous" means containers can hold different kinds of items. Therefore, HCCL provides a collection of list-like structures that are able to store different kinds of items. HCCL mitigates typing constraints in C++ since programmers are spared the task of implementing new container types for each new kind of object they develop.

More specifically, our container objects should have the following properties:

- *multiple occurrence* in the *same* container: the same object can appear many times in a container, for example, a has five occurrences in: (a b r a c a d a b r a);
- *multiple occurrences* in *different* containers: the same object can appear in any number of containers; for example, a occurs in: (a b r a c a d a b r a) and also in (a n y).
- *heterogeneity*: different kinds of objects can be included in a container; for example, the container (a "abc" 0) contains a character, a string, and a number.
- *multilevel* or *hierarchical* construction: containers that contain other containers as items can themselves be placed into containers; for example, the container ((a 0) (b 1)(c 2)) has three items each of which is a container.

HCCL was developed to enhance the C++ object-oriented programming (OOP) environment. One of the main advantages of OOP is that development time and effort can be greatly reduced through the use of reusable code. With such a facility, programmers no longer have to spend their time in coding something that is provided in a reusable library. This works well providing that code placed into a reusable library has been well tested. In this case, the only bugs introduced are those that arise from the new code built on the reused components.

C++ was chosen as the base language of HCCL because of its popularity. Although C++ has many OOP features, it also has its difficulties. One of the main limitations of C++ is caused by its strongly enforced typing conventions. (Interestingly, since Java shares C++ syntax and semantics, it has the same problems.) Objects of different types may not be treated interchangeably, or at the most, they may be interchanged only in very restricted ways. This situation is explained in the appendix to this chapter. Thus, support for keeping objects of different classes in the same container (heterogeneity) does not come naturally in C++. Although it is easy to implement a linked list in C++ to hold a single class of objects, it is not possible to implement a list to store heterogeneous objects directly. For advanced C++ programmers: generic pointers (pointer to void) cannot be used for this purpose. Although a list may be constructed with such pointers, there is no way to retrieve items from it, because generic pointer cannot be dereferenced. Moreover, a generic pointer has no way of knowing how much memory is required to store the information of an object that it points to.

Since there is no direct approach to implement a heterogeneous container, an indirect method has to be found to create a HCCL. There are eight main classes in HCCL: entity, element, pair, container, bag, set, relation, and function. However, only five of them are container classes. The rest of the classes, such as entity, element, and pair, serve as the auxiliary classes to build the containers. All of these classes are used to create objects with different but complementary behaviors.

6.1 HCCL Implementation Strategy

Figure 1 shows the implementation class hierarchy. Its structure differs somewhat from the behavior specification hierarchy in Chapter 5 to take advantage of the underlying sequential, pointer based processing of C++. As just said, the entity class will be the base class for all classes whose objects can go into containers. This sets up the basis for the heterogeniety property of containers we are aiming for. Our approach will very closely follow the "railway car" model implementation in Chapter 3. The class element is introduced to be provide the basic "cars" of the train (container). Using element also addresses the multiple occurrence property: different occurrences of the same entity can be placed in different elements. If we want to put an occurrence of an entity into a container, we merely construct a new element to hold the entity and string it into the container. Finally, by making container a subclass of entity, we enable container objects (trains) to be attached to elements (cars) and placed into other containers. This gives us the hierarchical construction capability, and hence all four properties we require.

Entity

The definition of class entity is sketched in Figure 2. Note that the entity name is protected (so that it is inaccessible and inherited that way too). There is a data member, classname, that is useful for testing equality. It is declared to be static, meaning that is shared by all instances of the class – this makes it a *class variable*. There are two constructors for entity, one of which takes the new entity's name as its argument. The destructor, ~entity(), frees up the memory space occupied by the instance for reuse. Print() and equal() are virtual since they are expected to be supplied by derived classes.

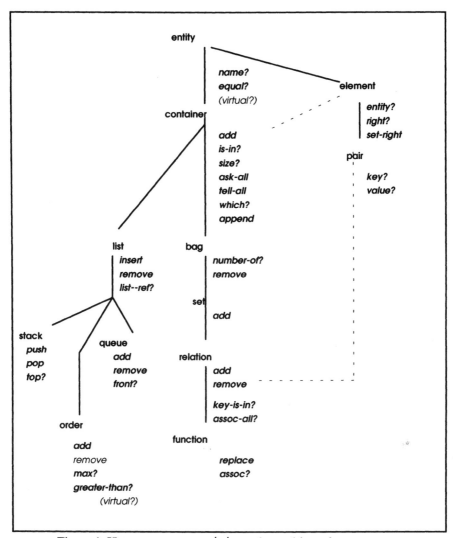

Figure 1. Heterogeneous container classes hierarchy.

All containers in HCCL use pointers to entity as the means to store objects. Therefore, to store an object it must directly or indirectly come from a derived class of class entity. Thus the key point to handling heterogeneous objects is to unify them under the umbrella of the entity class. In particular, since all of the classes in HCCL are derived from class entity, their instances may be stored in any HCCL containers. This leads to hierarchical construction, where containers may be placed into containers up to any level of recursion.

```
CLASS ENTITY

enum{FALSE,TRUE};  // FALSE = 0, TRUE = 1
typedef unsigned int Bool;

class entity {

private:

static char * classname;
   // used in testing of equality
protected:

char * name;          // name object

public:

entity ()
entity (char * NAME);
virtual ~ entity ();      //destructor
virtual void print()
   //print out the name of entity
virtual Book equal( entity * ent);
   //pointers comparison
virtual Book eq( entity * ent);
   //name fields comparison
};
```

Figure 2. Interface definition for entity (partial).

Element

Figure 3 sketches the interface for class element. As suggested above, there are two protected instance variables: ent, a pointer to an entity, and right, a pointer to an element. Public accessor methods are get_right(), get_ent() and set_right(element *). Print() and equal() for element invoke the same-named methods for the wrapped-up entity.

CLASS ELEMENT

```
class element : public { entity
private:

static char * classname;

protected:

entity * ent;          //pointer to entity wrapped within this element
element * right;       //link to the element on right

public:

element ();
element ( entity * ENT);
virtual ~ element ();
element *get_right();      //get the "right" (next) element for this object
entity *get_ent();         //get entity that of this element

void set_right( element *el); //link this element to another element
Bool equal( entity *ent);     //test for equality with he enclosed entity);
};
```

Figure 3. Interface definition for element (partial).

For example, the method equal is defined by

```
Bool element::equal(entity *ENT)
{
return (get_ent()->equal(ENT));
}
```

Although not apparent at first sight, the definition of equal is *progressive* – if the ent (returned by get_ent()) points to an instance of a derived class of entity, the equal method of the derived class will be invoked. This latter equal method may, in turn, call on one or more equal methods, and so on. Such invoking of the appropriate equal method is important for the correct functioning of such methods as is_in that rely on equal to do their work. We'll see examples of this phenomenon as we study the various container classes.

Container

Figure 4 outlines the definition of class container, the base class for all container classes. In line with the "railway cars" approach, there are two protected instance variables, head, a pointer to an element, and length. A picture of a typical container is shown in Figure 5.

```
CLASS CONTAINER:

class container : public entity
   { //so can be wrapped in element in
   //hierarchical container

private:
static char * classname;
protected:
int length;

element * head;

void add_first(element *el);  //add element at the first position
void add_at_head(element *el);     //insert element at head of list
void add_element (element *el);     //add element

public:

container ();
~container ();
void add(entity *ent);       //add object to the container
Bool is_in(entity *ent);      //is entity in the container?

int size();     //same as get_length
int get_length();     //get the lenght of list
Bool empty();       //is the container empty?
void print();       //print the items (recursively call their print())
```

Figure 4. Interface definition for containers (partial).

The public command add calls upon several private commands. It creates a new element to hold its argument, entity, as follows:

```
void add::add(entity *ent)
{
add_element(new element(ent));
}
```

elements are always added at the head, but the helper method add_element treats empty and non-empty cases distinctly:

```
void container::add_element *el)
{
  if (empty())
    add_first(el);
  else
    add_at_head(el);
}

void container::add_first(element *el)
{
  set_length(1);
  set_head(el);
}

void container::add_at_head(element *el)
{
  increment_length(1);
  el->set_right(head);
  set_head(el);
}
```

The method is_in(entity *) illustrates how to scan the elements in a container:

```
Bool add::is_in(entity * ent)
{
for (element *p = head;p != NULL;p = p->get_right())
if (p->get_ent()->equal(ent))
return TRUE;
return FALSE;
}
```

Note that the wrapped entity of each element is tested for equality with the entity in the argument. Since it is virtual, the equal method employed is that of the class of the wrapped entity; it has a **big effect** on the outcome.

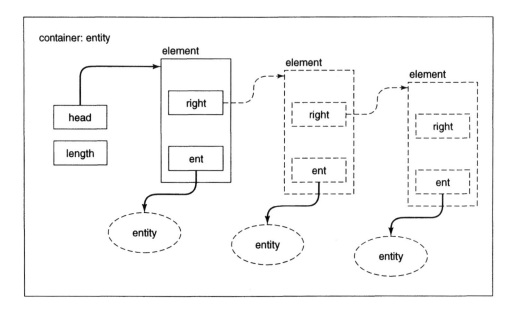

Figure 5. The internals of a container.

Bag

Recall that bags count the occurrences of included items. We also introduce the ability to remove items at this stage.

To get a count, we scan the container looking for wrapped entities that are equal to the one of interest:

```
int bag::number_of(entity *ent)
{
int num = 0;
for (element *p = get_head(); p != NULL; p = p->get_right())
if (p->equal(ent))
num++;
return num;
}
```

CLASS BAG

```
class bag: public container {
protected:

Bool is_head(entity *ent);      //check if it is a head element

element *previous(entity *ent);         //get to one element before the
                                        element w are looking for

void remove_head();          //remove the head element
void remove_middle(entity *ent);     //remove from the middle

public:

int number_of(entity *ent);   //how many ent occurences?
Void remove(entity *ent);

};
```

Figure 6. Interface definition for bag (partial).

The remove command has to consider several cases:

```
void bag::remove(entity *ent)
{
if(is_in(ent))
   if (is_head(ent))   // if it is the first element in list,
     remove_head();   // use remove_head() to perform
           // the deletion, else
     remove_middle(ent);// method to remove element
           // at middle of the list
}
```

The operation of the helper methods is similar to that in the "railway car" list removal command. We leave the details to the reader as an exercise (Problem 2).

Set

Class set is derived from class bag. It inherits all of bag's functionality and makes only one, major, modification. This is to allow entrance to at most one occurrence of the same object (Figure 7).

```
CLASS SET

class set: public bag{
public:
void add(entity *ent)
{
    if (!is_in(ent))        //if it is not already in set,
        container::add(ent);
                //add it using the inherited add method

}
};
```

Figure 7. Interface definition for set (partial).

Note that the global name of the container's add method is container::add. The prefixing of the class name avoids name clashes with methods with the same name in other classes.

Pair

Recall that mathematically, a *relation* is a *set* of *pairs*. So to define class relation we need to define class pair first. As shown in Figure 8, pair inherits an entity slot from element which can play the role of a key in a relation. We only have to introduce a second slot for a value.

Class pair has a constructor that accepts key and value arguments and packages them as a pair:

```
pair::pair(entity *KEY, entity *VALUE) : element (KEY)
{
value = VALUE;
}
```

CLASS PAIR

```
class pair: public element{
protected:
entity *value;          //consider inherited ent the key

public:
pair (entity *key, entity *VALUE);
Bool equal(entity *ent);
             //recursively check equality for both ent and value

};
```

Figure 8. Interface definition for pair (partial).

Recall the use of a base class constructor — element(KEY)– to work in a derived class constructor. Pair needs to override the inherited equal to test equality of its respective components. Pair's equal first tests that the argument entity's classname is its own ("pair"). Entities that are from different classes are certainly not equal. Moreover, if the classes are the same, then it makes sense to compare their respective keys and values (otherwise, the incoming entity may not have the value instance variable and a runtime error would result).

```
Bool pair::equal(entity *ENT)
{
return ( strcmp(get_classname(), ENT->get_classname()) == 0 &&
((pair *)ENT)->get_ent()->equal(get_ent())  &&
((pair *)ENT)->get_value())->equal(get_value()));
}
```

Relation

Figure 9 shows the main interface methods of class relation.

The add command of relation packages its arguments into a pair which it inserts using container's add. Note that set's query is_in and within this query, pair's equal are employed to check whether the pair is really a new combination of key and value worth adding.

```
void relation::add( entity *ent, entity *value )
{
pair *pr = new pair(ent, value);
if ( !(is_in(pr)) )
container::add_element(pr);
}
```

```
CLASS RELATION

class relation : public set {
public:

void add( entity *ent, entity *value );
Bool  key_is_in(entity *ent);
set *assoc_all( entity *ent );
void remove( entity *ent, entity *value );
set *range_objects();
set *domain_objects();

protected:
pair * next_key( entity *ent, pair *start );
};
```

Figure 9. Interface definition for relation (partial).

The helper method next_key is employed to search for a key required in the queries
key_is_in and assoc-all of relation.

```
pair *relation::next_key( entity *key, pair *start )
{
  if (start != NULL) {
for (pair *pr = start; pr->get_right() != NULL

                    && (!(pr->get_ent()->equal(key))));

  pr = ((pair *)pr)->get_right());
    if (pr->get_ent()->equal(key))
    return (pr);

  }

  return (NULL);
}

Bool relation::key_is_in(entity *key)
{
  return(next_key(key,(pair *)head) != NULL);
}
```

To collect all values associated with a given key, next_key is used until locations of key
are found.

```
set *relation::assoc_all(entity *key)
{
  pair *posn = (pair *)head;
  set *s = new set;

  while ( TRUE) {
    posn = next_key(key, posn);
    if (posn != NULL)
    {
      s->add(posn->get_value());
      posn = ((pair *)posn)_.get_right();
    } else
      return (s);
  }
}
```

To remove a key/value pair, relation's remove calls upon set's remove.

```
void relation::remove( entity *key, entity *value )
{
set::remove(new pair(key, value));
}
```

Function

Recall that a *function* is a relation for which at most one value is associated with any key. The two essentially new methods of function are shown in Figure 10.

CLASS FUNCTION

```
class function: public relation{

public:
void add(entity *ent, entity *value);
void replace(entity *ent, entity *value);
};
```

Figure 10. Interface definition for function (partial).

Function's add first checks whether the key in its argument is unpaired and if so, accepts the new key/value pair.

```
void function::add(entity *key, entity *value)
{
if (!key_is_in(key))
container::add_element(new pair(ent, value));
}
```

function's replace method looks for the pair matching the incoming key. If it finds it, it replaces the associated value by the new one. If the key is new, it calls upon the add command inherited from relation.

```
void function::replace(entity *key, entity *value)
{
pair *pr = next_key(key, (pair *)head);
if (pr != NULL)
pr->set_value(value);
 else add(key, value);
 }
```

6.2 Ensemble Methods in C++

The scanning illustrated in container's is_in method (Section 6.1) suggests how to implement the behavior of the ensemble methods tell-all, ask-all, and which? . However, in C++, it would seem that we have to write such methods individually for each use. For example, assume that a particular command has been defined for entity:

```
virtual void command();
```

and for derived classes of interest. Then we would write the following code to send this command to the items in a container:

```
void container::command_all()
{
for (element *p = get_head();p != NULL;p = p->get_right())
p->get_ent()->command();
}
```

Similarly, to broadcast a query to the container items and collect the results in a new container we would write

```
container * container::query_all()
{
container *c = new container();
for (element *p = get_head();p != NULL;p = p->get_right())
c->add( p->get_ent()->query() );
return c;
}
```

Although we have assumed that command and query have been declared virtual for entity, most methods will not satisfy this condition. One reason is that only a relatively small number were implemented when the entity class was defined. Another reason will be given in a moment. In the case where the method is not virtual, the extracted instance must be *cast down* to the particular class we are dealing with as discussed in an appendix to this chapter. For example, let vehicle be derived from entity. Then the effect of ask_all is obtained by

```
container * container::query_all()
{
container *c = new container();
for (element *p = get_head();p != NULL;p = p->get_right()){
   entity * ent = p->get_ent();  //pull off as entity
   vehicle * c = (vehicle *)c;   //note the cast down here
c->add(query() ;
}
return c;
}
```

Recall that which? extracts a container of items for which a boolean query returns TRUE. For a particular method boolean_query, this can be done:

```
container * container::which_boolean_query()
{
container *c = new container();
for (element *p = get_head();p != NULL;p = p->get_right())
if (p->get_ent()->boolean_query())
c->add( p );
return c;
}
```

where again boolean_query is assumed to be virtual for entity.

We come to the second reason why it may not make sense to declare the methods invoked in a scan to be virtual for entity. Consider a container of container objects (hierarchical construction). Define a method that will form a container of those container objects that have a particular item. Here we will use the container method is_in for which there is no equivalent in class entity. So even though is_in was known to be a method for container early in the implementation, we did not declare the is_in query as virtual since is_in has no intrinsic meaning for entity. Instead, we must cast down from entity to container as each item in the container is recovered:

```
container * container::which_is_in(entity * ent)
{
container *c = new container();
for (element *p = get_head();p != NULL;p = p->get_right())
   {
entity * e = p->get_ent();    //pull off as entity
container * vc = (container *)e; //cast down to container
if (vc->-is_in(ent))
c->add(vc);
return c;
}
```

Example: Ensemble Methods in C++

We revisit the example of Chapter 5 where containers of vowels and consonants were made and tested. First we create entities to represent letters:

```
entity * a = new entity("a");
```

...

```
entity * z = new entity("z");
```

To create vowels and consonants, we use bag as the most convenient class:

```
bag * vowels = new bag("vowels");
bag * consonants = new bag("consonants");
```

Add the letters to the right containers:

```
vowels->add(a);
```

...

```
vowels->add(y);

consonants->add(b);
```

...

```
consonants->add(z);
```

Call the method print() defined for bag:

```
vowels->print(); // (a e i o u y)
consonants-> print(); // (bcd .. xyz)
```

Collect all the letters in one container:

```
bag * letters = new bag();
letters->append(vowels);
letters->append(consonants);
cout << letters->size(); //prints 27
cout << letters->number_of(y); //prints 2
```

Create a container of bag instances:

```
container * partition = new container();
partition->add(vowels);
partition->add(consonants);
```

Test for vowel or consonant in one step:

```
container * results = partition->which_is_in(a);

        //see the above definition

    results-> print(); //prints ("vowels")

results = partition->which_is_in(b);
results-> print(); //prints ( "consonants");

results = partition->which_is_in(y);
results-> print(); //prints ("vowels", "consonants");
```

6.3 A Macro Approach to Ensemble Methods

Since we use the same basic code each time we need an ensemble action, there should be a way to have the computer write it for us. However, use of the *subroutine concept* will not work since the parts that need changing for specific applications are not acceptable as arguments. Instead, we can make use of the C++ preprocessor to rewrite our input text before it is compiled. The instructions to do this rewriting are called *macros*, several of which are listed in Figure 11 and shown in complete form in an appendix at the end of this chapter. Since macro writing is covered in basic C texts, we will limit this discussion to their application as ensemble methods.

```
.    copy(container1,class,container2)

·    tellall(container,class,command)
          Þ    tellall1(container,class,command,arg)
          Þ    tellall2(container,class,command,arg,arg1)


·    askall(container,class,query,results)
          Þ    askall1(container,class,query,arg,results)
          Þ    askall2(container,class,query,arg,arg1,results)


·    which(container,class,query,results)
          Þ    which1(container,class,query,arg,results)
          Þ    which2(container,class,query,arg,arg1,results)


·    which_not(container,class,query,results)
          Þ    which_not1(container,class,query,arg,results)
          Þ    which_not2(container,class,query,arg,arg1,results)


·    whichone(container,class,query,result)
          Þ    whichone1(container,class,query,arg1,result)
          Þ    whichone2(container,class,query,arg1,arg2,result)
```

Figure 11. Macros for ensemble methods.

copy(container1, class,container2)

> where

- container1 is an existing instance of a container class,
- class is the name of the class to which each instance will be cast down,
- container2 is another existing container instance.

copy is a slightly more general form than append in that it casts down the entities in the first container into the specified class before appending them to the receiving container.

tellall(container,class,command)

> where

- container is an existing instance of a container class,
- class is the name of the class to which each instance will be cast down,
- command is the method that will be applied to each instance.

We can use this macro to implement tell-all functionality. For example,

> tellall(vowels,entity,print);

tells each entity in vowels to print its name. Note that in this case, no casting down is actually needed, but it does no harm to do it.

To implement ask-all functionality, we need to set up a container of results first:

askall(container,class,query,results)

> where

- container is an existing instance of a container class,
- class is the name of the class to which each instance will be cast down,
- query is the method that will be applied to each instance,
- results is an existing instance of a container class.

For example, we can ask all vowels to return their names to a container of names:

```
container * names = new container();
askall(vowels,entity,get_name, names);
names->print(); //prints aeiouy
```

The existing macros accommodate up to two arguments. For example, the functionality of the which? ensemble method using a query with one argument is given by

which1(container,class,query,arg,,results)

> where

- container is an existing instance of a container class
- class is the name of the class to which each instance will be cast down
- query is the method that will be applied to each instance
- arg is the only argument of query
- results is an existing instance of a container class

Note that we need to write a different macro for each desired number of arguments (although fortunately, not for their types). Thus, macros which, which1 and which2 have been defined to handle zero, one, and two arguments, respectively. Rarely do query or command methods require more than two arguments.

Typically, we package these macros within specific methods. For example, we can define the method which_is_in with less work than required in the original implementation:

```
container * container::which_is_in(entity * ent)
{
    container *c = new container();
    which1(this,container,is_in,ent,c);
    return c;
}
```

A final example will show how to obtain the which-one functionality. Here, we need a pointer to hold the single result of the selection:

```
whichone1(container,class,query,arg,result)
```

where

- container is an existing instance of a container class,
- class is the name of the class to which each instance will be cast down,
- query is the method that will be applied to each instance,
- arg is the only argument of query,
- result is an existing instance of class.

For example, we can define a method to return the item with a desired name:

```
entity * conainer::which_one_has_name(char * nm){
entity * res = new entity();
whichone1(this,entity,eq,nm,res);
return res;

}
```

Appendix 1: Ensemble Method Macros

```
#define defptr() element *p;

#define copy(source,class,dest) \
defptr()\
 for (p = source->get_head();p != NULL;p = p->get_right())\
   dest->add((class *)(p->get_ent()))

#define tellall(cont,class,command) \
defptr()\
 for (p = cont->get_head();p != NULL;p = p->get_right())\
    ((class *)(p->get_ent()))->command()

#define tellall1(cont,class,command,arg) \
defptr()\
 for (p = cont->get_head();p != NULL;p = p->get_right())\
    ((class *)(p->get_ent()))->command(arg)

#define tellall2(cont,class,command,arg,arg1) \
defptr()\
 for (p = cont->get_head();p != NULL;p = p->get_right())\
    ((class *)(p->get_ent()))->command(arg,arg1)

#define askall(cont,class,query,results) \
defptr()\
 for (p = cont->get_head();p != NULL;p = p->get_right())\
    results->add(((class *)(p->get_ent()))->query())

#define askall1(cont,class,query,arg,results) \
defptr()\
 for (p = cont->get_head();p != NULL;p = p->get_right())\
    results->add(((class *)(p->get_ent()))->query(arg))

#define askall2(cont,class,query,arg,arg1,results) \
defptr()\
 for (p = cont->get_head();p != NULL;p = p->get_right())\
    results->add(((class *)(p->get_ent()))->query(arg,arg1))

#define which(cont,class,query,results) \
defptr()\
 for (p = cont->get_head();p != NULL;p = p->get_right())\
    if (((class *)(p->get_ent()))->query())\
      results->add(p->get_ent())

#define which1(cont,class,query,arg,results) \
defptr()\
 for (p = cont->get_head();p != NULL;p = p->get_right())\
```

```
        if ((((class *)(p->get_ent()))->query(arg))\
            results->add(p->get_ent())


#define which2(cont,class,query,arg,arg1,results) \
defptr()\
  for (p = cont->get_head();p != NULL;p = p->get_right())\
      if ((((class *)(p->get_ent()))->query(arg,arg1))\
          results->add(p->get_ent())


#define which_not(cont,class,query,results) \
defptr()\
  for (p = cont->get_head();p != NULL;p = p->get_right())\
      if (!(((class *)(p->get_ent()))->query())\
          results->add(p->get_ent())


#define which_not1(cont,class,query,arg,results) \
defptr()\
  for (p = cont->get_head();p != NULL;p = p->get_right())\
      if (!(((class *)(p->get_ent()))->query(arg))\
          results->add(p->get_ent())


#define which_not2(cont,class,query,arg,arg1,results) \
defptr()\
  for (p = cont->get_head();p != NULL;p = p->get_right())\
      if (!(((class *)(p->get_ent()))->query(arg,arg1))\
          results->add(p->get_ent())



#define whichone(cont,class,query,result) \
defptr()\
  for (p = cont->get_head();p != NULL;p = p->get_right())\
      if ((((class *)(p->get_ent()))->query())\
          result = p->get_ent()


#define whichone1(cont,class,query,arg1,result) \
defptr()\
  for (p = cont->get_head();p != NULL;p = p->get_right())\
      if ((((class *)(p->get_ent()))->query(arg1))\
          result = p->get_ent()


#define whichone2(cont,class,query,arg1,arg2,result) \
defptr()\
  for (p = cont->get_head();p != NULL;p = p->get_right())\
      if ((((class *)(p->get_ent()))->query(arg1,arg2))\
          result = p->get_ent()
```

Appendix 2: C++ Typing Rules That Arise From Inheritance

Since C++ requires that all slots (variables) be typed, we cannot arbitrarily assign instances of classes to slots. Many errors occur at run time when a message sent to a slot does not match the method repertoire of its current occupant. The C++ compiler can prevent many of such runtime errors by disallowing certain assignments at compile time. These assignments relate to base/derived class compatibilities. Consider for example, Figure 12 which illustrates the following (sketchy) class definitions:

```
class airplane: public vehicle{};

class tank: public vehicle{};
```

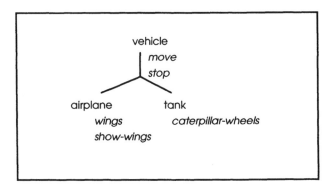

Figure 12. Class hierarchy for vehicle.

Figure 12 shows the inheritance hierarchy we are assuming, with vehicle as a base class to derived classes tank and airplane. Consider declaring variables v,a, and t as pointers to vehicles, airplanes, and tanks respectively. Let's assign them the addresses to new instance of their corresponding classes at the same time:

```
vehicle * v = new vehicle();
airplane * a = new airplane();
tank * t = new tank();
```

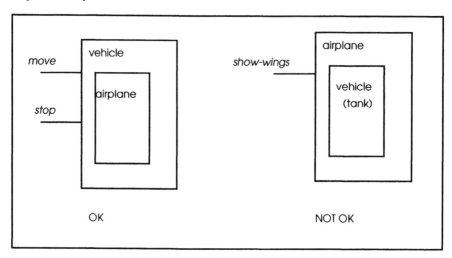

Figure 13 Typing restrictions in C++

Figure 13 illustrates the following typing rules:

- Assignment of a subclass (derived) instance to a superclass (base) slot is allowed by the compiler:

    v = t; //put tank in vehicle slot --allowed by compiler

- The reverse assignment (of a superclass instance to a subclass slot) is not allowed:

    t = v; //attempt to put vehicle in tank slot -- not allowed by compiler

To understand why we need to outlaw assigning base instances to derived class slots, assume such a law is not enforced. Then consider the sequence:

    v = t; // put tank in vehicle slot - ok

With the law unenforced we can put vehicle into airplane slot:

    a = v; //assume this is not prohibited

Now send the airplane slot a message it should be able to handle:

    a->show_wings();

But it can't , since it is currently holding a tank in disguise (see Figure 13).

In other words, vehicles can't be put into airplane slots since they don't always have the specific features that are assumed for airplanes.

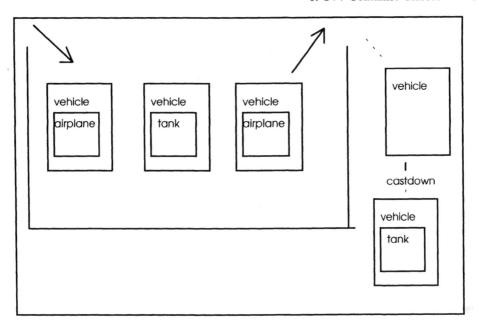

Figure 14. Illustrating type casting constraints.

The compiler allows the occupant of a slot to receive only messages that belong to the class that has been declared for that slot. Thus, methods that are specific to a derived class (i.e., that are not defined for the base class) will not be accepted in a base class slot. For example, since v has been declared to be of type vehicle:

    v->move();

is allowed by compiler, but since show-wings is not a feature of vehicles:
    v->show-wings();

is not allowed. Once again, the reason is easy to see when we imagine that a tank might have been assigned to v and it would then not be able to respond to airplane messages. These typing rules have important implications for designing heterogeneous container classes.

Strong typing presents challenges relating to both adding and removing. Figure 14 illustrates these problems. First of all, the argument of the add method must be as general as we need to make it to encompass all the classes of objects that we intend to place in the container. Second, when removing an object from the container, the compiler knows only that it is of the generic base type (e.g., vehicle) that has been declared upon entry. So we have to use our knowledge of the situation to tell the compiler exactly what subclass (e.g., airplane) the object really is. This is called *casting down*.

For example, if we know that the object that we have picked and assigned to v is really an airplane, then the casting operation looks like

a = (airplane *)v

This assigns to slot a the address that v holds along with the information that the layout of the object for airplanes should be used when interpreting messages sent to v. The cast down can be done in one step, as in

((airplane *)v) ->show_wing();

Note the enclosing parentheses which say that v is to be cast, not
v->show_wings(), the compiler's natural interpretation.

Since we are interested in containers that can hold arbitrary types of objects, we create a class called entity intended to be the base class for any user defined class. This means that if you want to use such containers, you must

1. always derive your classes from entity (directly or indirectly) and

2. remember to cast down the type of an extracted item to the particular type capable of receiving the messages you want to send it..

Virtuality and Dynamic Binding

Returning to vehicles, airplanes and tanks, consider a method such as move() that has been defined for the base class, vehicles. By inheritance, each of the following would invoke the same version of move(), namely, that of vehicles:

```
v->move();
a->move();
t->move();
```

Now suppose that airplanes overrides the inherited version with its own version of move():

```
class airplane: public vehicle{

public:

void move(){...}

};
```

The situation now is

```
v->move(); //invokes vehicle::move()

a->move(); //invokes airplane::move()

t->move(); //invokes vehicle::move()
```

But what happens after assigning airplane in a to v? Look at

```
v = a;
v->move(); //still invokes vehicle::move()
```

Since the compiler recognizes only the type of v which has been declared as vehicle, it invokes the method for vehicle as before. Knowledge of the type of the occupant of the slot v can be gained only at run time. The compiler must be told to offload this decision to the run-time system if we want the proper version of the method to be called. To cause this run-time processing to occur, we must declare a method to be virtual in the base class:

```
class vehicle{
public:
virtual void move(){...}
}
```

The situation

```
v = a;
v->move(); // invokes airplane::move()
```

now unfolds as we expect. The run-time system checks the class of the current occupant of v and invokes the code for the method of that class. The information required for this processing is placed into a table, called the *virtual function table*, associated with the base class.

The virtual concept suggests another consequence for using containers in C++: we must declare methods that all subclasses of entity will use (such as print(), and equal()) to be *virtual* for base class entity. This is an essential condition for heterogeneity: – when the run-time system examines each object in a container, it can tell which version of a virtual method to apply to it.

Problems

1. We can nondestructively append one container to another by

    ```
    void container::append(container * c)
    {
    for (element *p = c->get_head();p != NULL;p = p->get_right())
    add(p->get_ent());
    }
    ```

    Explain what would happen if add_element(p) were to replace

    add(p->get_ent())

2. Write and test the helper functions for bag removal. Hint: use the helper methods:

    ```
    Bool is_head(entity *ent);
    element *previous(entity *ent);
    void remove_head();
    void remove_list();
    void remove_middle(entity *ent);
    ```

3. Class relation's queries, domain_objects and range_objects, return sets of all keys and all values used in a relation's key-value pairs. Define these query methods in C++..

4. Implement class list as a derived class of container in C++. (Hint: one way to do it is to keep the natural order given by pointer linkage and to count to get to the desired position. For example, list_ref(i), starting at the head, counts up to i while advancing to the right.)

5. *(Memory Management)* C++ does not reclaim memory space automatically when an object is no longer usable (has no references to it) although it offers the programmer some convenient means to do so. Although beyond our scope we mention that classes have destructors that can be used to free up the memory held by an instance. However, the problem facing the C++ programmer is to avoid sending messages to an object that has been destroyed. With this in mind, design a derived class of entity that keeps track of all references to an instance and allows destruction only at the last reference. (Hint: use a class variable which maintains a bag of references and their occurrences. The declaration looks like:

    ```
    class en: public entity{
    private:
    static bag * m;
    public:
    en(char * nm):entity(nm);
    ```

```
en * make_copy();// use when adding a new reference.
        //~en(); don't use a destructor
void release();  //use instead. Calls the destructor at the last moment.
int number_of(); //number of references to this entity in central bag
};
```

An example of use (although trivialized is:)

```
main(){
en* a = new en("a");
en* b = a->make_copy();
en* c = a->make_copy();
en* d = a->make_copy();
a->release();
b->release();
c ->release();
d ->release();
}
}
)
```

6. (Methods for Hierarchical Containers) Define method print() for class container that
    prints the names of the entities in a container; for any entity that is also a container,
    it recursively applies the print() method. (Hint: use polymorphism and virtual
    definition of print.)

    Discuss a general approach to defining recursive methods for hierarchically con-
    structed containers.

7
Testing Based on Behavior Specification

While "getting it right the first time" is an admirable goal, no one is able to write code that is guaranteed to work as intended without testing and debugging. *Testing* is the process of uncovering errors or "bugs" in code. *Debugging* is the process of removing them. The many books on object-oriented programming, C++ and Java in particular, tend not to deal with these issues. Books on software engineering do discuss testing as an important phase within software system development, but a good approach to testing that is tuned to the special characteristics of object orientation is not yet available. This chapter will provide the beginnings of such an approach that emerges naturally from the concepts of behavior specification that we have developed.

This methodology should attempt (or even guarantee) to produce a test suite that is as *thorough* as time and money allow. A failed test should output the *behavioral aspect* it was aimed at, thus providing a useful starting point for the debugging process. The test suite should be able to *evolve* as the software system evolves, making sure each update or release maintains the levels of performance achieved in the past.

7.1 The Look-and-See Method

Before proceeding with a systematic approach to testing, let's first consider one we might adopt called "look-and-see." In the method "look-and-see," after writing the code for a class, you create an instance of it and apply a method to it. This is the "look" part. You then see if the code runs and that the results are what you expect them to be. If not, you try to find out what's wrong and correct it. After you've finished debugging this method, you apply a second method to the instance. You continue in this manner until you are satisfied that the code is working as expected.

There are three major **problems** with this haphazard and idiosyncratic approach:

- *Thoroughness*: in all this looking and seeing there is no guarantee that you are looking in the right place for errors. Chances are that you are examining a part of the overall behavior that you personally are aware of. Other users, however, and this includes you later, will rarely be familiar with the assumptions you made and will attempt to use the class in ways you did not think of. The behavior they will be seeing will not have been tested and will probably be buggy.

- *Repeatability*: debugging often introduces new bugs, so there is no guarantee that tests that were passed earlier will still be satisfied. So you really need to repeat all earlier tests after every code fix. Moreover, these tests need to be repeated for later reimplementations of the same behavior. Subsequent modifications of the behavior may be able to reuse many of the same tests.
- *Self-disclosure*: the test results should be in the form of a binary decision, pass/fail, not requiring you, or later someone else, to stare at the output for a while before deciding whether or not it is correct and which part of the behavior it was addressing.

In contrast, a systematic approach would attempt to produce a test suite that is as thorough as possible. Such a test suite could be reapplied as needed and produce crisp pass/fail results. Having tangible form, a test suite would be open to improvement as new conditions are discovered or to adaptation as new modifications are made.

7.2 Testing Rudiments

Some of the basic requirements for a systematic test methodology are easily met. Tests should be expressed in the language the software is written in and stored in files that can be compiled if necessary and executed. Every class should have an associated test file. Tests should provide crisp pass/fail results and document the underlying purpose. Here's an example of such a test in C++:

```
cout << "TESTING IF NAME IS PROPERLY SET BY ENTITY CONSTRUCTOR" << endl;

entity * e = new entity("trial");
if (strcmp(e->get_name(),"trial") == 0)
    cout << "test satisfied";
    cout << "test NOT satisfied";
```

Such tests can be entered into a file whose name associates to the name of the class under test. For example, the file "testentity.C" contains a sequence of tests such as the one just given. This test file was executed many times before the initial version of the entity class stabilized. Now, whenever there is modification to the "entity.h" or "entity.C" file (and there always seems to be a new reason for an enhancement!), "testentity.C" is modified, if necessary, and recompiled and executed to make sure the new code has not been inadvertently corrupted.

Testing is by nature a tedious process. Tools can be developed to minimize the routine drudgery. For example, a class Test can be defined that supports testing C++ classes. Figure 1 illustrates the use of this class in a file that tests the container class.

```
main(){

Test * ConTest = new Test; //make a new instance of Test for this class

ConTest->ShowInfo("Container Tests","container.h container.C","container");

                    // print out relevant information
entity *book = new entity("book");
ConTest->Print(1, "Creating new entity called book...");
ConTest->Exists(book);        //was book successfully created

container * con1 = new container;
ConTest->Print(1, "Creating new container con1 with no name ...");
ConTest->Exists(con1);

ConTest->Series("container::add() & container::is_in()");
         //start a series of tests concerning add and is_in

ConTest->Focus("container::empty()");
                   //within above series, focus on empty()
ConTest->Is_Equal("con1 empty? ", con1->empty(), TRUE);
              // output "test passed" if container is empty
              // otherwise "test NOT passed"

ConTest->Focus("container::size()");
ConTest->Is_Equal("con1's size is 0? ", con1->size(), 0);

ConTest->Focus("container::add(entity *) & container::is_in");
con1->add(book);
ConTest->Is_Equal("book is added, is con1 holding book now ? ",
              con1->is_in(book), TRUE);

// more focal tests in this series
// additional series

ConTest->Report(); // report the test result statistics:
                   // how many series were done,
              // how many tests were done, how many were in error
}
```

Figure 1. An example (partial) of a test file using class test.

Note that Test supports documenting tests and their purposes, comparing query outputs with expected values, and automatically tallying test results. Figure 2 shows some the output of the test of an early version of the container class. We can see at a glance at the end of the printout that there were tests that failed, and then by scanning the file we can easily identify which ones they were. In the early stages, however, a full printout is most likely **not** to be had! Many "crashes" occur that halt execution. Worse, the run-time system may give little or no indication of the cause of the crash. Segmentation faults are a notorious example: access was attempted to an undefined pointer—but which one was it? In such cases, the point at which printing stopped provides useful information since the point of failure must have occurred after it. In contrast, look-and-see testing of a complex program may result in a crash and offer no clue as to what caused it.

```
----------
ShowInfo:
----------

Title      : Container Tests
Test on File : container.h container.C
Test Class  : container
----------


Creating new entity book ...
Object entity exists.

Creating new container con1 with no name ...
Object container exists.


-------------------------------------------------
container::add() & container::is_in() tests series
-------------------------------------------------

Test Focus: container::empty()
con1 empty? : True
Test passed.

Test Focus: container::size()
con1's size is 0? : True
Test passed.

Test Focus: container::add(entity *)
              & container::is_in(entity *)
book is added, and is in con1? : False
Test NOT passed.
.......

Report:
----------

Total Series  : 7
Total Test    : 25
Error Detected :5
----------
```

Figure 2. Output from test file (partial).

7.3 Blueprint-Based Testing

Rudimentary test-supporting tools are fine, but they only raise new questions. How do we determine what series of tests to run? How do we come up with the purpose of each test and then implement it? How many tests are enough?

For some insight, let's return to the diagram in Chapter 5 in which the "blueprint," the object behavior specification, formed the center of all interaction among designer, implementor, tester, and user (see Figure 3). A blueprint for a class, if *complete and consistent*, specifies exactly the behavior expected from the objects in this class. How the designer can provide a complete and consistent blueprint has been a main consideration until this point. Now, we focus on the guidance that the blueprint can offer in developing tests for a class.

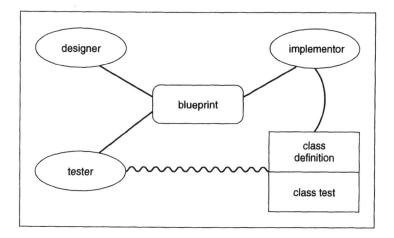

Figure 3. Software Blueprint as a contract between designer, implementor and tester.

As pictured in Figure 3, the class specification for code development can be viewed as a contract between the implementor and the tester. The implementor agrees to bring the blueprint to life. The tester agrees to ascertain whether the living beast conforms to the blueprint specification — nothing more nor less. To fulfill her side of the bargain, the implementor supplies a class definition. To discharge his responsibility, the tester provides a test suite. *Both class definition and test suite are based on the blueprint and are developed independently of each other and in parallel.* When both are ready, they are combined into one executable file and the results observed. The reason they can be developed independently is that all the behavior to be expected from the implementation is specified in the blueprint, including the names of the methods and the types of their arguments. Realistically, the object behavior specification we have discussed does not provide lower-level details, such as whether a number is to be integer or floating point, or other considerations that are specific to the implementation language. So some adjustment is needed to make the tests match the class definition. But since the basic interface specification has been agreed to (in the blueprint), the adjustment needed is relatively minor.

This is all well and good in the abstract, but practically speaking, how can the tester translate the blueprint into a concrete suite of tests? First, let's recall *that the behavior of an object is the set of all the query-terminated sequences of commands that can be applied to it together with their responses.* Mathematically, the behavior of a class is a *relation* where each pair consists of a legal query-terminated sequence of commands as key and the value is that returned by a newly constructed instance. One way to go about testing, therefore, is to list each legal query-terminated sequence of commands in a file and check whether the actual response agrees with the value dictated by the behavior specification. The tests we illustrated earlier for the entity and container classes fit this form.

7.4 Constructing Behavior Samples

In general, there are an infinite number of pairs in the behavior relation, so we can only *sample* a finite set of these pairs in a practical test suite. The question now is: how to choose such a sample? It would be nice if I could offer you an algorithm that took a behavior specification and automatically generated a finite subset of tests that was as thorough as can be within some prescribed limits of time and money. Unfortunately, such an algorithm cannot exist. However, there are two approaches we'll discuss that can go some distance toward the goal exemplified by such an algorithm. The first approach focuses on the intended functionality of the class — out of all the numerous legal query-terminated sequence of commands, which ones represent normal scenarios intended for the users?

Normal Behavior Example: Testing the Alarm Class

We have previously specified the alarm class behavior and discussed its application to a house alarm system. Let's see how an alarm implementation would be tested, focusing on its normal behavior.

For convenience, we recall its object behavior specification (Figure 4).

constructor

alarm make-alarm(key)

queries

boolean armed?(alarm) //is the alarm set to work?
boolean open?(alarm) // is the door (or window) open?
boolean sound?(alarm) // is the alarm screeching?

hidden

key key?(alarm) // what is the required key?

commands

alarm' arm(alarm,key) //set the alarm to work using the proper key
alarm' disarm(alarm,key) //turn off the alarm using the proper key
alarm' open(alarm) // open the door
alarm' close(alarm) // close the door

Equivalences

armed?(make-alarm(key)) = F
open?(make-alarm(key)) = F
sound?(make-alarm(key)) = F
key?(make-alarm(key)) = key

open?(alarm) = F & key?(alarm) = key =>armed?(arm(alarm,key)) = T
armed?(arm(alarm,key)) = F
                          // only applies when above condition fails
key?(alarm) = key => armed?(disarm(alarm,key)) = F
armed?(disarm(alarm,key)) = armed?(alarm)

armed?(open(alarm))) = F
armed?(close(alarm)) = armed?(alarm)

open?(arm(alarm,key)) = open?(alarm)
open?(disarm(alarm,key)) = open?(alarm)
open?(open(alarm)) = T
open?(close(alarm)) = F

sound?(arm(alarm,key)) = sound?(alarm)
key = key?(alarm) => sound?(disarm(alarm,key)) = F
sound?(disarm(alarm,key)) = sound?(alarm)
                // only applies when above condition fails
armed?(alarm) = T => sound?(open(alarm)) = T
sound?(open(alarm))= sound?(alarm)
                // only applies when above condition fails
sound?(close(alarm)) = sound?(alarm)

Figure 4. Object behavior specification for class alarm.

The main function of the alarm is to sound when it is armed and a break-in occurs. Thus, if the alarm is armed with the right key and the door is subsequently opened, we want the alarm to sound.

The following query-terminated sequence and response correspond to this scenario:

```
alarm = make-alarm(key1)
alarm' = arm(alarm,key1)
alarm'' = open(alarm')
sound?(alarm'')= T
```

Somebody knowing the right key should be able to get in by disarming the alarm:

```
alarm = make-alarm(key1)
alarm' = arm(alarm,key1)
alarm'' = disarm(alarm',key1)
sound?(alarm'') = F
```

But not knowing the proper key, a burglar will not be able to disarm the alarm and it will still warn of a break-in:

```
alarm = make-alarm(key1)
alarm' = arm(alarm,key1)
alarm'' = disarm(alarm',key2)
alarm''' = open(alarm'')
sound?(alarm''') = T
```

These query-terminated sequences represent normal user scenarios for the alarm, and its proper response is critical to its existence. However, there are many other possible sequences that might arise in practice that must be tested.

The following query-terminated sequence corresponds to arming the alarm with the wrong key and subsequently opening the door; does the alarm sound?

```
alarm = make-alarm(key1)
alarm' = arm(alarm,key2)
alarm'' = open(alarm')
sound?(alarm'') = ?
```

The following query-terminated sequence corresponds to arming the alarm with the right key,subsequently opening the door; then closing the door; can the alarm be armed?

```
alarm = make-alarm(key1)
alarm' = arm(alarm,key1)
alarm'' = open(alarm')
alarm''' = close(alarm'')
alarm^{iv} = arm(alarm''',key1)
armed?(alarm^{iv}) = ?
```

The following query-terminated sequence corresponds to arming the alarm with the right key, subsequently opening the door, then forgetting to close the door; can the alarm be armed?

```
alarm = make-alarm(key1)
alarm' = arm(alarm,key1)
alarm'' = open(alarm')
alarm''' = arm(alarm'',key1)
armed?(alarm''') = ?
```

Since the behavior specification is complete and consistent, each of the above responses can be worked out by simulation. Clearly, we should test for them and as many other scenarios that might arise as possible. In general, we must try to conjure the many unintended scenarios that the user is apt to get into. But is there any way of knowing if all the scenarios have been considered? No, but our second approach can guarantee that all "aspects" of the behavior have been considered. By "aspects" we mean *query/command* pairs, or equivalently, state transitions, as we will see in a moment.

7.5 Testing Constructors for Correct Initialization

Before proceeding with the query/command pairs, let's note that the *query/constructor* pairs in the object behavior specification provide the information for defining constructors and testing that they work properly. For example, the query/constructor pairs for class alarm are:

```
armed?(make-alarm(key)) = F
open?(make-alarm(key)) = F
sound?(make-alarm(key)) = F
key?(make-alarm(key)) = key
```

They can be tested in a series of the form:

```
alarm * a = new alarm("key1");
AlarmTest->Is_Equal("a armed? ", a->armed_q(), FALSE);
AlarmTest->Is_Equal("a open? ", a->open_q(), FALSE);
AlarmTest->Is_Equal("a sound? ", a->sound_q(), FALSE);
AlarmTest->Is_Equal("a key? ", a->key_q(), "key1");
```

Since key? is a hidden query, we should treat it differently, as we discuss later.

7.6 State Transition–based Testing

Earlier in Chapter 2, we recognized that objects are state machines (although not necessarily finite state machines). To fully test such a system obviously requires that we test the transitions and outputs of the object in each of its states. The state equations in an object behavior specification provide the information we need to do such testing. Recall that a complete specification contains all combinations of state representing queries and commands. For example, in the alarm class, there are 4 queries and 4 commands, so there are 16 query/command combinations. Each such query/command pair describes the effect of the command in changing the state as "seen" by the query. Each pair, therefore, represents an **aspect** of the object behavior that is independent from all the others. Thus, a thorough test suite must include at least one test of each query/command pair. However, the more tests we do of each aspect of behavior, the more opportunity to expose its bugs. So we should try to test each query/command pair on as many states of the object as time and money allow. Since an alarm object has a finite number of states, we can create an alarm instance for each state and apply each query/command pair to each instance.

The alarm class has three state-representing queries: armed?, open? and sounding?. (The query key? is not supposed to change once initialized, so we don' t count it for this purpose.) Each returns a boolean value, so there are at most $2^3 = 8$ states (not all of which might be reachable from the initial state, as we will discuss later). Assuming the implementation uses instance variables armed, open, and sounding, let's make eight instances, each in a different state.

    alarm * alarm1   = new alarm (/* armed */F,/* open */F,/* sounding */F,/* key */"key1")
    alarm * alarm2   = new alarm (/* armed */T,/* open */F,/* sounding */F,/* key */"key1")
    alarm * alarm3   = new alarm (/* armed */F,/* open */T,/* sounding */F,/* key */"key1")
    alarm * alarm4   = new alarm (/* armed */T,/* open */T,/* sounding */F,/* key */"key1")
    alarm * alarm5   = new alarm (/* armed */F,/* open */F,/* sounding */T,/* key */"key1")
    alarm * alarm6   = new alarm (/* armed */T,/* open */F,/* sounding */T,/* key */"key1")
    alarm * alarm7   = new alarm (/* armed */F,/* open */T,/* sounding */T,/* key */"key1")
    alarm * alarm8   = new alarm (/* armed */T,/* open */T,/* sounding */T,/* key */"key1")

Now we write tests for the 16 query/command pairs. We'll return later to consider this more fully, but to illustrate, let's write two easy ones. The equation

    armed?(open(alarm)) = F

can be readily transformed to the method

```
alarm::armed_q_on_open(){
open();
return armed_q() == T;
}
```

The equation

```
armed?(close(alarm)) = armed?(alarm)
```

states that the armed state is not affected by closing the door and is transformed into

```
Bool alarm::armed_q_on_open(){
Bool * old_alarmed = armed_q();
close();
return armed_q() == old_alarmed;
}
```

After writing the tests for the 16 query/command pairs, we apply each test to the 8 test instances. For example, for the pair armed?-on-open, we have:

```
test (alarm1->armed_q_on_open);
test (alarm2->armed_q_on_open);
...
test (alarm8->armed_q_on_open);
```

where Test prints "test satisfied" if its argument is true and "test NOT satisfied" otherwise.

Since the instances alarm1,...,alarm8 are modified by the focal command, we need to recreate a new set of fresh instances for each test. Thus for example,

```
alarm * alarm1  = new alarm (/* armed */F,/* open */F,/* sounding */F,/* key
*/"key1")

...

alarm * alarm8  = new alarm (/* armed */T,/* open */T,/* sounding */T,/* key
*/"key1")
```

```
test (alarm1->armed_q_on_close);
test (alarm2->armed_q_on_close);
...
    test (alarm8->armed_q_on_close);
```

depicts the section relating to the armed?-on-close. All in all, we have a file containing at least 16 test functions each applied to 8 fresh instances, for a total of 128 pass/fail tests.

7.7 Transition-Based Test Methodology

While the state transition-based testing approach can generate a thorough test suite, it clearly needs tool support to reduce the tedium and drudgery involved (not to mention, the errors that might be introduced in the tests themselves due to this drudgery). Before returning to the dangling threads of the last section, this section introduces methodology and tools in C++ that greatly reduce, but do not entirely eliminate, the work needed in transition-based testing. Before describing the tools, consider the main steps of the methodology:

1. Write test methods for each query/command equation in the object behavior description,
2. Form a container of these test methods,
3. Form a container of instance makers in different states,
4. Apply each test method to each instance (freshly reconstituted as necessary),
5. Form a container of test results showing the pairs of tests and instances they failed on.

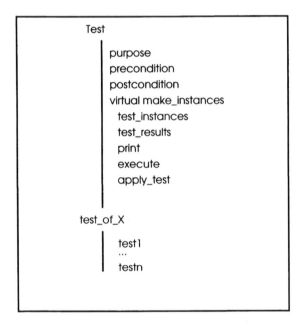

Figure 5. Transition test framework.

Figure 5 shows a framework for supporting this methodology. To test a class X , we define a define a subclass, test_of_X of class Test . For example,

```
class test_of_alarm:public Test{};
```

The methods of this class will implement the tests developed from the object behavior specification. Class Test has four instance variables whose roles are illustrated in the following prototype method description:

```
Bool test_of_X ::query_on_command(X * test_instance){

............ ;// local constants to be used for

        // arguments and tests

purpose = ............ ;//description of test objective

precondition = ........;// condition that must be

        //satisfied by test instance

test_instance-> ........;// command sent to test instance

postcondition = ............ ; // condition that should

        //be true after commands

}
```

For example, consider the equations for query/command pair, armed?/arm. For the first rule,

```
open?(alarm) = F & key?(alarm) = key
        => armed?(arm(alarm,key)) = T
```

we write

```
test_of_alarm::armed_q_on_arm1(){
char * key = "key1";
purpose = "test if alarm can be armed under proper conditions";
precondition = !test-instance>open_q() &&
    test_instance->key_q() = key;

test_instance>arm(key);
postcondition = test-instance>armed_q();
)
```

Note that the precondition corresponds to the "if" part of the rule, while the postcondition represents the "then" part. In general, a rule in the behavior specification has the form

$$precondition \Rightarrow postcondition$$

though in many rules the precondition is only implicitly there. For example, the second rule,

```
armed?(arm(alarm,key)) = F
```

only applies when the previous rule does not. Thus, its explicit form is:

```
not(open?(alarm) = F & key?(alarm) = key)
    =>armed?(arm(alarm,key)) = F
```

Thus, this rule is translated as

```
Bool test_of_alarm::armed_q_on_arm2(){
char * key = "key1";
Bool complement = test-instance>open_q() &&
    test_instance->key_q() ==key;

purpose = "test if alarm rejects arming under right conditions";
precondition = !complement;
test_instance>arm(key);
postcondition = !test-instance>armed_q();
)
```

Many rules are *unconditional*, which means their precondition is always true. For example,

```
armed?(open(alarm)) = F
```

is translated as

```
Bool test_of_alarm::armed_q_on_open(){
purpose = "test if alarm always is not armed after open";
precondition = T;
test_instance>open();
postcondition = !test-instance>armed_q();
)
```

Similarly,

```
armed?(close(alarm)) = armed?(alarm)
```

is translated as

```
Bool test_of_alarm::armed_q_on_close(){
Bool old_armed = test_instance->armed_q();
purpose = "test if close does not affect alarm armed state";
precondition = T;
```

```
test_instance>close();
postcondition = test-instance>armed_q() == old_armed;
)
```

Note the definition of a local variable, old_armed to hold the value returned by armed? before sending the arm command. The rule says that this value should not change.

Step 3 in the methodology calls for providing "instance makers" that can be called to generate fresh copies of instances. This is illustrated in Figure 6.

```
class test_of_alarm:public Test{

public:

test_of_ alarm():Test(){}

void make_instances() {

test_instances = new set;

alarm * alarm1  = new alarm (/* armed */F,/* open */F,/* sounding */F,/* key
*/"key1");

test_instances->add(alarm1);

    ...

alarm * alarm8  = new alarm (/* armed */T,/* open */T,/* sounding */T,/* key
*/"key1");

test_instances->add(alarm8);

}
```

Figure 6. Generating test instances.

For each test developed as above, we write a corresponding method for class test_of_alarm that uses a macro to apply the test to each of the test instances. For example, for the test

```
test_of_alarm::armed_q_on_arm1
```

we write the method:

```
void test_of_alarm::armed_q_on_arm1_all(){
apply_test(armed_q_on_arm1);
}
```

We then write an executable file that invokes each of the tests on all the instances:

```
int main(){
test_of_alarm * t = new test_of_alarm();
t-> armed_q_on_arm1_all();
t-> armed_q_on_arm2_all();
t-> armed_q_on_open_all();
t-> armed_q_on_close_all();
t->print();
}
```

The results appear in the form of an instance of test_result, which is an instance of class function, holding for each failure-detecting method the container of failed instances. For example, the print-out,

((armed_q_on_arm1 (a2 a5)) (open_q_on_arm (a1)))

indicates that armed_q_on_arm1 failed on instances a2 and a5 while open_q_on_arm failed on a1. All other tests passed or were not applicable. To see how this is done, let's look at the code for the method execute which is automatically called after applying a test method:

```
Bool Test::execute(){
cout << purpose;
if (!precondition) {
    cout << ": test not applicable" << endl;
    return TRUE; }
else if (postcondition) {
    cout << ": test satisfied" << endl;
    return TRUE;    }
    else {
cout << ": test NOT satisfied" << endl;
return FALSE;
}
```

Note that a test is not applicable when the precondition is false. For example, armed_q_on_arm2 cannot be applied to alarm instance a3 since a closed door is needed to set the alarm. If the precondition is true and the postcondition is also true, the test is satisfied. Otherwise (when the test is applicable but the postcondition is false), the test fails. Note, that the method returns FALSE only in the last case, since we want to know only about applicable tests that failed.

7.8 Transition-Based Testing: More Considerations

We'll apply the transition-based test methodology to class set to illustrate some useful tips. Consider defining class test_of_set:

```
class test_of_set: public Test{
...
};
```

Incorporating Domain Restrictions in Preconditions

Recall the restriction on removal expressed by

remove(set,entity) = defined provided that

is-in?(set,entity) = T

In testing the equations for the pair is-in?/remove in the set behavior specification

is-in?(remove(set,entity),entity)) = F

we can incorporate this domain restriction into the precondition:

```
test_of_set::is_not_in_on_remove(){
entity * a = new entity("a");
purpose = "test that item is not there after removing it");
precondition = test_instance-> is_in( a);
test_instance-> remove (a);
postcondition = !test_instance->is-in(a);
)
```

This will prevent trying to remove an item that is not in the set. More generally, we should incorporate the domain restrictions of a specification into the precondition of any test for which it is relevant.

Refining Tests by Splitting Preconditions

There should be no effect of removing one item on the inclusion status of another:

is-in?(remove(set,entity),entity1)) = is-in?(set,entity1)

The test for this is straightforward:

```
test_of_set::still_is_in_on_remove(){
```

```
entity * a = new entity("a");
entity * b = new entity("b");
Bool old_is_in = test_instance->name_is_in(b);
purpose = "test that item is still there after removing another");
precondition = test_instance-> is_in( a);
test_instance-> remove (a);
postcondition = test_instance->name_is_in(b) == old_is_in ;
)
```

However, if this test were to fail, we would not know whether it was because an existing entity was accidentally removed or because a new entity was accidentally added in. A little foresight can make it easier to diagnose problems such as this by splitting the possibilities as different tests. In this case, we can have two tests corresponding to the initial value of old-is-in .

The first tests for the case of an existing item:

```
test_of_set::still_is_in_on_remove(){
entity * a = new entity("a");
entity * b = new entity("b");

purpose = "test that item is still there after removing another");

precondition = test_instance-> is_in( a) && test_instance-> is_in( b);

test_instance-> remove (a);

postcondition = test_instance->name_is_in(b);

}
```

The second tests for introduction of a new item:

```
test_of_set::still_is_in_on_remove(){

entity * a = new entity("a");

entity * b = new entity("b");

purpose = "test that item is still there after removing another";

precondition = test_instance-> is_in( a) && !test_instance-> is_in( b) ;

test_instance-> remove (a);

postcondition = test_instance->name_is_in(b) == F;

)
```

Another reason to split tests is to increase the sensitivity to boundary states that could be sources of error. For example, we might split the test for is-in?/add into 3 regions of set size: 0, 1, and > 1.

```
test_of_set::is_in_on_add0(){

...

precondition = test_instance->size() == 0;

...

test_of_set::is_in_on_add1(){

...

precondition = test_instance->size() == 1;

...

test_of_set::is_in_on_add2(){

...

precondition = test_instance->size() > 1;

...
```

For a set with a limited capacity, we might include tests that are sensitive to the sizes near and at the maximum.

Making Test Instances

Recall that test instances represent different states of an object. The approach of constructing such states by assigning values to instance variables depends on knowing what these are and having a general constructor that has arguments for all these variables. Moreover, such state combinations may not actually be of interest in that they may not be reachable by any legal sequence of commands. *To make our test instance makers generic we can limit state construction to those states accessible by sequences of commands.* Even more efficiently, in many cases, we can limit the commands used to a subset that can construct all legal states. For example, a list is most directly constructed from a sequence of insert commands (although we could also use remove methods, the same effect can be achieved with just insert commands alone).

How Many Test Instances Are Enough?

In a relatively small finite state system such as alarms, it is feasible to completely cover the state space with test instances. However, this may not be feasible for a large state space or if the state space is infinite, as in the case of container classes. The guiding principle here must be to cover the *tests* rather than the states. In other words, *use enough test instances so that every test is applicable at least once.* Of course, within the limits of time and money, the more test instances, the better. It is easy to arrange minimal test coverage — for each test, we make a test instance that will apply to that test. Of course, a major advantage of using test-all is that all tests are tried on all instances, so a test instance might accommodate many more tests that it was designed for. Since the burden of test-suite thoroughness is now on the tests, we should be *zealous in splitting tests* where there is a real advantage to doing so, as just discussed.

However, there are times when splitting tests is not enough and we have to add more instances. An example is illustrated in the alarm test armed?-on-arm2. Here, the precondition looks like

```
!(!test_instance->open_q() && test_instance->key_q() == key)
```

By Demorgan's law, this transforms into a disjunction of the basic conditions:

```
test_instance->open_q() | | test_instance->key_q() != key
```

The test will be applicable if either of the basic conditions is true. So the test will apply to any instance with an open door, *independently* of the input key. But, we would also like to test to make sure that the alarm doesn't get set when the input key is *incorrect.* So we should split the test into two: one with the precondition

```
test_instance->open_q()
```

and one with precondition,

```
test_instance->key_q() != key
```

But to cover the second test, we need to make at least two instances that differ in their key settings. Thus, where preconditions can be put into disjunctive form, we can split tests and make sure there are enough instances so that each can be tested (see the Problems).

Opening Up the Black Box

To characterize behavior using the state equation approach is it often necessary to add queries to properly represent the state. When they are not properly part of the public interface, such state-representing queries are marked "hidden" in the specification. In implementations, such queries might become instance variables or methods and in C++ they would be qualified as "private" (or "protected") and therefore not accessible for use in the test methods. Not being able to use these queries might severely limit testability. For example in class *alarm*, not being able to query for the hidden *key* would prevent us from testing the arming and disarming methods. Thus, we have to "open up the black box", that is, extend the public interface, for testing purposes while making sure that its original form prevails for actual use. There are several ways to do this in C++.

A straightforward solution is to add special access methods to the public interface. For example,

```
class alarm{

  public:

   int get_key();

   ...

 }
```

The problem then is resisting the temptation to use these special methods for other than testing purposes. Of course, we should impose a stricture against such use. Unfortunately, this stricture would not be enforceable by C++ itself since we declared the access methods to be public.

A more secure approach is to use the concept of friend in C++. We can make the test class a friend of the class under test:

```
class alarm{

 friend class test_of_alarm;

   ...

 }
```

This gives test_of_alarm direct access to all accessible methods and instance variables of alarm without exposing them to other clients.

7.9 Combining the Approaches

In general, a test suite should contain

1. tests that constructors work properly: these come from the part of the object behavior specification that involve query/constructor pairs,

2. samples of query-terminated sequences that characterize normal and abnormal scenarios,

3. tests based on query/command pairs in the object behavior specification and test instances to cover them.

Problems

1. Using the Test class in C++, write a test file for the alarm class based on the normal and abnormal behavior query-terminated sequences identified in the chapter.

2. Using the state-transition approach, write a test suite for the class pair as specified below:

   ```
   pair inherit from entity
   constructor
   pair make-pair(key,value)
   queries
   entity key?(pair)
   entity value?(pair)

   commands
   pair' set-key(pair,entity)
   pair' set-value(pair,entity)

   Equivalences:
   key?(make-pair(key,value) = key
   value?(make-pair(key,value) = value

   key?(set-key(pair,entity)) = entity
   value?(set-key(pair,entity)) = value?(pair)

   key?(set-value(pair,entity)) = key?(pair)
   value?(set-value(pair,entity)) = entity
   ```

3. Write a specification for the cross product of two containers. A pair is in this cross product just in case its key entity is in the first container and its value entity is in the second container. Using the state-transition approach, write a test suite for this class.

4. Write a specification for the test methodology implemented by the class hierarchy in Figure 5. For example, the final testing process can be represented by

   ```
   is-in?(container-of-test-methods,query?) = T

     & is-in?(container-of-test-instances,entity) = T

     & query?(entity) = F

         => is-in?(container-of-results,query?,test-instance) = T
   ```

5. Refine the test suite for alarms by splitting armed?-on-arm2 into two tests and add an additional test instance to provide for applicability requirements.

6. Write a behavior specification and test suite for the n-counter class (see Problems, Chapter 1) in C++. Compare the approach of adding public methods intended only for testing purposes with that of making the test class a friend of the n-counter class.

7. a) Write a behavior specification for the def state machine introduced in the Problems of Chapter 1.

b) Assume that a class def has been defined in C++ using method names is_defined, set, and clear. Now define a class var whose instances each encapsulate a single variable and use def to keep track and control the definition of that variable, as in the following:

```
class var{
private:
 int value;
  //assume that only non-negative integers are used
 def * d;
public:
var();
void set( int val );
  // sets the value if allowed by d otherwise has no effect
int get_val();
  // gets the value if defined according to d, otherwise returns -1
void reset();
  // clears the def instance
};
```

c) Write a test suite for testing class var based on the methodology in this chapter.

8
Constructing Inheritance Class Hierarchies

In this chapter we formulate a heuristic procedure that can produce an inheritance class hierarchy. The procedure is *heuristic* since we don't spell out how to make key decisions, such as finding common features for a group of classes. These decisions have to be made based on your knowledge of the application domain.

8.1 How to Construct Inheritance Hierarchies

Let's suppose that you have a collection of classes in mind already and are seeking to organize them to take the most advantage of commonalities using inheritance. For example, you might know that investments can be made in a number of different ways and have formulated these ways as classes, such as various kinds of stocks, bonds, and ways to earn money from savings. After discussing the procedure for constructing a class hierarchy, we show how class variables and ensemble methods are useful in implementing the resulting system.

Inheritance Hierarchy Construction Procedure

Start with classes of interest := all the classes under consideration. Loop until all classes under consideration have been assigned a place in the hierarchy:

1. Analyze the behaviors of the classes of interest, looking for features that are common to them all.
2. Define a root class to contain the common features just identified
3. Divide the classes of interest into groups, where each group consists of classes with many features in common
4. For classes that seem not to fall into any of the groups just identified, let them be derived from the root class
5. For each group, let it be called the classes of interest and recursively apply the procedure above (starting from step 1) to each such group. The root class formulated for each group is the subclass introduced to capture the common features of that group.

In practice, you may not be able to formulate all the classes of interest explicitly. For example, you may know that investments come in the form of stocks, bonds, and bank accounts, but have not further elaborated these major divisions. The above procedure is still applicable in that it encourages you to discover what features are common to group classes and what features differentiate them. The common features are incorporated into a subclass at the next level. Along the way, you may find that a division you originally thought was a good one (e.g., breaking bonds into municipal bonds and federal bonds) would be better replaced by another division that exhibited more commonality (e.g., bonds might be better broken up into short-term and long-term yielding bonds).

8.2 Class Hierarchy Example: Investments

We now examine a system that enables investors to assess the quality of potential investments. We will use this example to illustrate the heuristic procedure for constructing an inheritance class hierarchy. The investments will be represented by object classes. The methods of the classes must be able to apply the specific knowledge needed for determining how good investments are in these classes. After constructing the hierarchy, we will show how containers and ensemble methods can be used to organize groups of investments called portfolios and compute their money-earning potential.

Figure 1 shows the investment class hierarchy. The features common to all investments are placed in the root-level investment class. It is made a subclass of entity so that its instances can be placed into containers. We then break up investments into stocks, bonds, and bank accounts, which all have a lot in common and are quite distinct from each other. We continue this process at the next level. For example, the features that are common to all stocks are placed in the class stock, and then the different types of stocks are categorized in fairly homogenous classes such as blue chip and high-technology stocks. Of course, many more subclasses would be differentiated in a real investment application design.

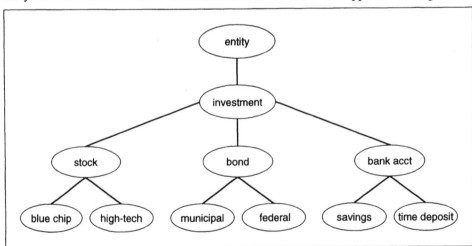

Figure 1. Investment class hierarchy.

Figure 2 shows how the root class – the most general class – investment is specified. Every class in the hierarchy will inherit methods such as get_name inherited from entity and compute_quality . But note that the method for computing quality may differ quite drastically for each class. Each class will use its own characteristic attributes, as represented by its instance variables, and specific formulas or other procedures, to compute such a quality figure.

```
define class: investment
    methods:
        get_name(inherited from entity)
        compute_quantity (virtual)
    inheritance: entity
```

Figure 2. Investment class specification.

Next-level classes stock, bond, and bank_acct are specified in Figure 3. Notice that each has a different selection of instance variables that are pertinent to assessing the quality of its type of investment. For example stock uses *price:earnings* ratio while bond uses *value_at_maturity* among other similar attributes. While such attributes and means to employ them are different, the end result as returned by compute_quality has the same meaning. This is the essence of ***information hiding*** (how the computation is done is hidden within the object) and ***polymorphism*** (different classes provide different definitions for the method with the same name intended to perform similar behaviors).

Further specializations of the major classes are defined in Figure 4. As shown, such specializations provide characteristic default values for the instance variables inherited from the parent class. However, a specialized class may ***override*** the inherited method for computing quality in favor of a more appropriate one of its own. In this case, all further specializations of this class will inherit this method.

```
define class: stock
instance variables:
 price:earnings
 growth potential
 dividend potential
methods:
     compute_quality
        return estimate based on factors
                        embodied in instance variables
        inheritance: investment
```

```
define class: bond
instance variables:
 value at maturity
 rating
 maturity period
 methods:
 compute_quality
     return estimate based on factors
                    embodied in instance variables
inheritance: investment
```

```
define class: bank acct
instance variables
 interest rate
methods:
     compute_quality
     return estimate based on factors
                        embodied in instance variables
     inheritance: investment
```

Figure 3. Specializations of the major classes.

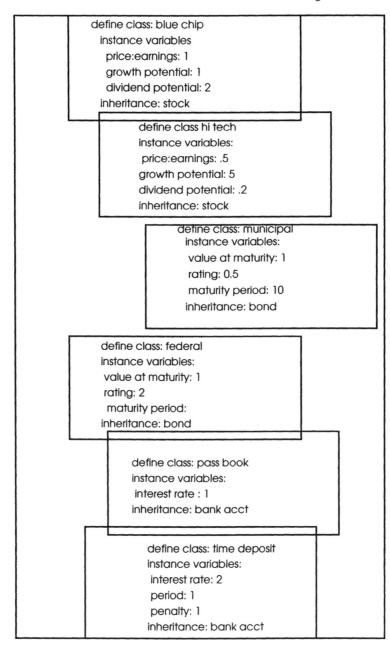

Figure 4. Next-level specialized classes of investments.

8.3 Portfolio Selection and Rating Specification

Let's consider a system that enables users to assess the quality of a portfolio of investments. Such a portfolio is a container of investment objects which users can construct and then evaluate. The user may experiment with variations, removing and adding investments, until satisfied that a best selection has been made. Compute_total_quality for a portfolio sums up the qualities of each of the investment objects in it. These values are obtained by asking each investment the message to compute its own quality using ensemble methods.

A specification of the portfolio selection and rating system is shown in Figure 5.

```
portfolio: a container of instances of investments
                                and its specialized classes

Method: select (portfolio):

        for each investment in the container of investments
            query the user whether to add this investment


Method: adjust(portfolio)

        for each investment in portfolio
            query the user whether to remove this investment


Method: show(portfolio)

        for each investment in portfolio
            send investment display information


Method: compute_total quality(portfolio)

        total := 0

        for each investment in portfolio
            send investment compute_quality
            add result to total

        return total
```

Figure 5. Specification for portfolio selection and rating.

To illustrate the desired operation, let's create a few investment instances:

```
make_investment(blue_chips ibm with price:earnings .75)
make_investment (blue_chips at&t with price:earnings .70)
```

make_investment (hi_techs inferco with growth potential 10)
make_investment (hi_techs intel with growth potential 5)
make_investment (municipals tucson_city_bond)
make_investment (federals us_bond)
make_investment (pass_books valley_sav)
make_investment (time_deposits valley_time)

The user selects a subset of such investments, or portfolio, using select. These can be displayed using show; for example:

show(portfolio) -> (ibm intel us_bond)

Then, by applying compute_total_quality to this portfolio, an estimate of its quality is obtained. To further experiment with the portfolio, the user might use adjust to add or remove investment objects.

Notice that once these methods are implemented, they should not have to be modified later as new classes of investments are added. These methods only assume that any object they examine will have appropriate methods such as compute_quality, but they are not concerned about what lies hidden beneath such interfaces.

8.4 Implementing the Investment System

Having the HCCL class library at our disposal puts us in a good position to implement the portfolio selection and rating system. Basically, there are two types of containers needed: one that holds all investments and one for portfolios. Since only one copy of investments is needed, we can use a global variable to hold an instance of container. Even better, we can restrict direct access to such a variable to the instances of investment by defining it to be a *class variable* of investment. A *class variable* differs from an *instance variable* in that it can be directly read and written by any instance of the class (whereas an instance variable is local to each instance of the class). As we have seen, in C++ a class variable is declared using the qualifier static. In this context we have

```
class investment: public entity{
protected:
static set * investments;
...
}
```

Such a class variable needs to be initialized outside the class definition, as in

```
investment::investments = new set();
```

Then it can be accessed directly within class methods:

```
investment::investment(char *nm):entity(nm){
investments->add(this);
}
```

Since there may be more than one portfolio, we define a class portfolio. Figure 6 shows how some methods of portfolio, which form the desired interface, call upon related methods in class investment.

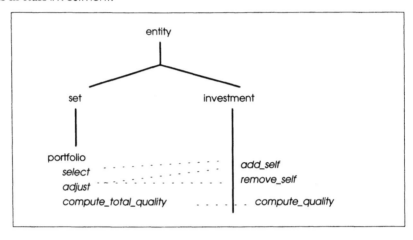

Figure 6. Portfolio methods invoke investment methods.

The methods of class portfolio employ ensemble macros. Only a few statements are needed to realize the desired behavior:

```
class portfolio: public set{
...
}

portfolio::select(){
tellall1(investment::investments,add_self, this);
}

portfolio::adjust(){
tellall1(this,remove_self,this);
}

portfolio::compute_total_quality(){
total(this,total_quality);
)
```

Similarly, it is straightforward to realize the various subclasses of investment. For example, the stock class take the form:

```
class stock: public investment{
private:
price_earnings_ratio
growth_potential
dividend_potential

...
}

stock::stock(char * nm):investment(nm){}
stock::compute_quality(){
return price_earnings_ratio *
    growth_potential * dividend_potential;
}
```

8.5 Polymorphism and Dynamic Binding

In accord with polymorphism, each subclass can have its own version of compute_quality. *Dynamic binding* enables porfolio's methods that call on virtual methods of investments to work no matter which subclasses of investments are present. For example, suppose a porfolio, p contains the objects: ibm at&t intel us_bond valley_sav. Then consider the processing required in compute_total_quality:

```
p->compute_total_quality()
```

calls on the ensemble method ask-all:

```
ask-all p compute_quality()
```

which is expanded to:

```
ibm->compute_quality()
```

```
at&t-> compute_quality()
```

```
intel-> compute_quality()
```

```
us_bond->compute_quality()
```

```
valley_sav->compute_quality()
```

Note that the classes of the objects differ, and since compute_quality is virtual, its behavior depends on the class. Thus, the C++ run-time system must recognize the class to which it belongs and use the appropriate code for computing quality. This is called *dynamic* binding as opposed to *static* binding, which can be done at compile time. This contrasts to the case of a nonvirtual method such as show-self. Here the same code is used no matter what the class of the object, so dynamic binding is unnecessary. Recall that C++ can exploit such *static* binding, since it considers it as the default unless virtual is declared. Other languages, Java in particular, work with dynamic binding exclusively. Whether polymorphism requires static or dynamic binding, the fact remains that it supports **extensibility** — for example, new classes of investments can be easily added and compute_total_quality will continue to work without modification provided that each new class has a compute_quality method — either inherited or specially defined.

8.6 Extensibility

A major advantage of inheritance is that a hierarchy of classes does not have to remain fixed once and for all, but can continue to evolve as the need for new classes arises. The ideal case for such *extensibility* is where you only need to add a new class by finding a proper place for it in the hierarchy. The best place is where it can inherit the most features from a superclass, leaf number to be modified or added. For example, a new form of savings plan might fit well under bank_acct, while investment in real estate might need to be formulated as a new class under investment. A less ideal case is where we have to modify the definition of an existing class. The effects of this modification will then propagate down to all its subclasses. This more radical alteration might be avoided by coming up with a good hierarchy in the first place, following the hierarchy construction procedure discussed at the beginning of this chapter.

Problems

1. Draw the investment class behavior hierarchy showing the classes, their subclass relationships, and methods. Implement the investment class and its subclasses in C++. Prepare for your implementation by drawing the C++ implementation class hierarchy. For methods to compute quality, consult with someone knowledgeable, read a book, or make up some formulas based on your intuitive understanding.

2. Add a new class of investments to the hierarchy. Choose the best level at which to add this new class. (Hint: decide this on the basis of how many features can be inherited from the potential superclass versus how many features have to be modified or added).

3. An investment company has created the following class hierarchy:

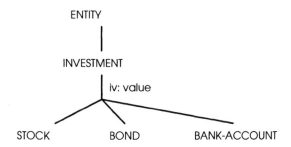

Using Ensemble methods define the following:

investment::show_all_investments()

investment::show_all_stocks()

investment::show_all_bonds()

investment::show_all_bank_accounts()

Investors purchase individual stocks, bonds or bank accounts, and place these objects in sets called portfolios. In other words, portfolio is derived from set:

Using ensemble methods, define the following:

```
set * portfolio::get_investments_greater_than (n){
// returns the subset all investment objects in portfolio with value greater than n

...
}
void portfolio::deduct_charges(){
// decreases value of each investment object in portfolio by
// calling each investment's method deduct_charges

...
)
```

Define the investment methods assumed in the above:

```
boolean investment::greater_than (n){

...
}
void investment::deduct_charges(){
//reduces value by an amount determined differently in each subclass
// default is reduction by %5

...
}

void stock::deduct_charges(){

...
    }
```

```
void bond::deduct_charges(){
...
}
void bank_account::deduct_charges(){
...
}
```

4. Using the heuristic procedure in this chapter, develop a class hierarchy for employees of a company you are familiar with. Employ a class variable to keep track of all employee instances created. Develop methods to compute the salaries of employees that take full advantage of the hierarchy's inheritance properties.

5. Consider the following class specialization hierarchy:

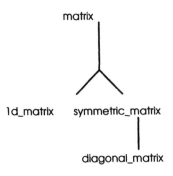

where matrix is a class of n by n matrices. For concreteness, we will assume that n = 2; so the displayed form is:

a11 a12
a21 a22

- symmetric_matrix is a class of symmetric 2 by 2 matrices, i.e., a12 = a21,
- diagonal_matrix is a class of diagonal 2 by 2 matrices, i.e., a12 = a21 = 0 and,
- 1d_matrix is a class of one dimensional matrices, i.e., a11 = a21 = a22 = 0 (a12 is not zero)

Consider methods for each of the following.

1. transpose() interchanges a12 and a21,
2. compute-determinant() returns the determinant of the matrix represented by A
3. compute-trace() returns the trace of the matrix represented by A (i.e., a11 + a22).

4. multiply_vector(v) applies the matrix to the vector represented by v and returns the resulting vector (v is a pair (v1, v2)).

5. print() prints out the matrix in the manner above, i.e.,
   a11 a12
   a21 a22

Each of these methods can be inherited from the base class. However for efficiency of computation, it is better to override the inherited method in some of the classes. Place a check mark ξ in the following table for each case in which the inherited method should be overridden. Provide an explanation if you believe that the answer depends on assumptions.

method	matrix	symmetric_ matrix	diagonal _matrix	1d_matrix
transpose	x			
compute _determinant	x			
compute_trace	x			
multiply_vector	x			
print	x			

9
Ensemble-Based Implementation of Containers

In earlier chapters, we discovered primitives for list implementation in serial computers. Historically, these pointer-based primitives were the first to be developed. But with the advent of parallel processing, and in view of new technologies likely to emerge for computation, we should not be limited to the conventional primitives. Ensemble methods are very suited to exploit parallel computation. This chapter shows that the ensemble methods for containers can serve as primitives for implementing all the behaviors of the containers' hierarchy that we have identified.

To be more specific we will show how the methods of all container subclasses can be implemented using only ensemble methods and a small number of ordinary methods. Moreover, we will not allow ourselves to use any information about containers' internal structure. In the language of C++, containers must serve as a *private* base class for any derived class. Working within this constraint forces us to be very explicit in our implementation. We can't use anything about a container's behavior that is not provided by the external interface. To implement a behavior, we must use only ensemble methods and introduce any new helping methods explicitly. The end result helps us to understand what basic functionality must be provided by an implementation in a new language, platform, or technology.

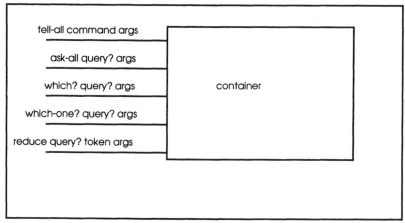

Figure 1. Ensemble methods of container.

9.1 More Ensemble Methods

The three ensemble methods already discussed are depicted in
Figure 1, along with two new ones. Recall the original methods

- tell-all command args – send the command(args) message to all objects in the container,
- ask-all query? args – send the query?(args) message to all objects in the container and collect the results in a returned container (see Figure 2).
- which? query? args – send the query?(args) message to all objects in the container and collect objects returning TRUE in a new container.

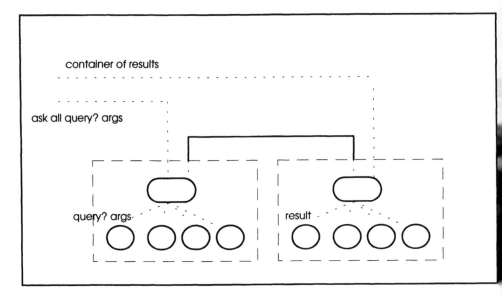

Figure 2. The ensemble method ask-al.

We add two new methods:

- which-one? query? args – return the one entity in which? query? args provided there is exactly one; otherwise return an unspecified entity in which? query? args.
- reduce query? token args – pass the token from object to object in the container in an unspecifed order. Each successive object replaces the token with the results of query?(token,args). After all replacements are done, the token is the final result returned.

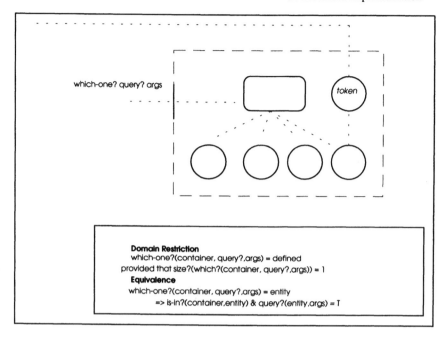

Figure 3. Illustrating the which-one? ensemble method.

Which-one?

Which-one? (Figure 3) is a variant of which?. If there is a unique entity in a container that satisfies a query then which-one? returns this entity. However, the specification does not specify which particular item in the container is returned (of those that satisfy the query) in case more than one such entity exist. Specifications such this one, which do not specify a unique outcome are called **non-deterministic**. An implementation of such a specification must somehow make a decision if there are multiple choices. Such a choice might be based, for example, on the first satisfactory item encountered in some order of examination. Of course, the result may very well depend on the order chosen.

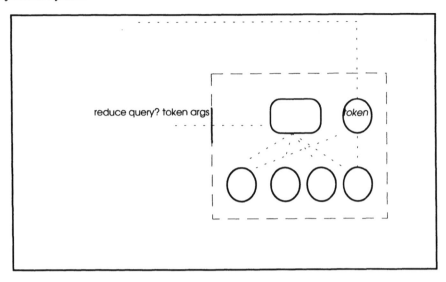

Figure 4. The ensemble method reduce.

Reduction

Reduce (Figure 4) is similar to which-one? in that it returns a single entity rather than a container. Figure 5 gives the specification.

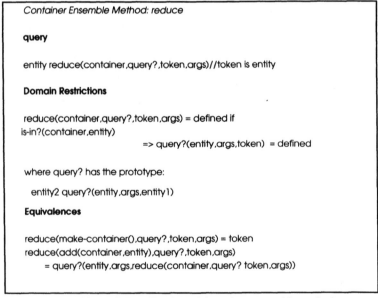

Figure 5. Specification of the reduce ensemble method.

For example, let's total up the numbers in a container (assume we have a class number that will be defined later). Then,

number2 plus?(number,number1)

fits the prototype of the query in Figure 5, where

plus?(number(x),number(y)) = number(x+y)[1]

Let's make a container with three numbers:

c = make-container()
c' = add(make-container(),number(x))
c'' = add(c',number(y))
c''' = add(c'',number(z))

and define the token as:

token = number(0)

Since reduction of an empty container just returns the token:

reduce(c,plus?,token) = number(0).

Also reduction applied to a just-added entity applies the query to it and the previous reduction. Thus

reduce(add(c,number(x)),plus?,token)
   = plus?(number(x),reduce(c,plus?,token))
   = plus?(number(x), number(0))
   = number(x)

Continuing on in this way

reduce(c'',plus?,token)
   = reduce(add(c',number(y)),plus?,token)
   = plus?(number(y), reduce(c',plus?,token))
   = plus?(number(y),number(x))
 = number(x+y)

and

---

[1] Number(x) is a constructor with numerical argument x

```
reduce(c''',plus?,token)
   = reduce(add(c'',number(z)),plus?,token)
    = plus?(number(z), reduce(c'',plus?,token))
    = plus?(number(z),number(x+y))
= number(x+y+z)
```

Actually, reduce can be synthesized from tell-all. For example, given a query that accepts and returns an instance of the same class, we can define another method that tells each entity in container to apply the query to a token and return it as a result, thus implementing reduce for that query (see the Problems).[2] Although it can be synthesized in each application, the general concept of reducing a container to an entity is worthy of embodying in a new ensemble method. Such a method is applicable to many computations. For example, finding the maximum or minimum of a collection of numbers are examples of reduction (see the Problems).

9.2 Implementing Container Classes by Ensemble Methods

Figure 6 shows the hierarchy of container classes as implemented using an ensemble-based approach. The methods shown below the dotted lines are implemented using the methods appearing above the dotted lines. The (latter) primitive methods can be enumerated as follows:

- the methods belonging to classes entity[3] and pair,
- the basic methods, size? and add, and ensemble methods of class container,
- the method remove of class bag, and
- the methods of class number (needed for ordered container classes).

---

[2] Note that, as specified, reduce produces a well defined value since computation follows the history of addition of entities to the container. However, in implementation, this history will usually not be known so that properties of the binary operation, query?, must justify order independence. The properties of associativity and commutativity are sufficient for this purpose.

[3] Except for add-self and remove-self.

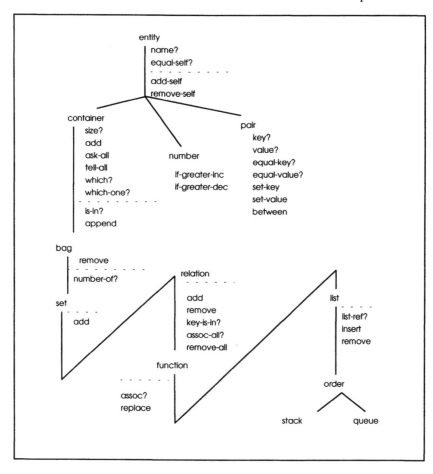

Figure 6. Ensemble-based implementation hierarchy for container classes.

Let's see how the methods of container and its subclasses are implemented using the primitives only. First we shall implement the *unordered* container classes. It is quite straightforward to implement lists and the other *ordered* classes once having implemented class function.

Container's methods synthesis

Since add and size? are primitives, is-in? is the only basic method requiring synthesis. To find out whether an item is in a container using ensemble methods, we ask each item if it is the one being sought. If any affirmative replies are received, we have an affirmative answer.

is-in?(container, entity) =

  not(empty?(which?(container,equal-self?,entity)))

Observe that which? collects the entities equal to the input entity. We then test whether the resulting collection is empty?. Recall that empty? is derivable from size?.
To synthesize append we make use of add-self defined for entity:

  add-self(entity, container) = add(container, entity)

  append(container,container1) =
    tell-all(container1, add-self, container)

Thus all the nonprimitive methods of container can be synthesized using which? and tell-all of container and equal-self? of entity.

Bag's Methods Synthesis

We need to synthesize number-of? (the only new query introduced by class bag); bag's number-of? can be synthesized in a manner to similar to that used in is-in? of container:

  number-of?(bag,entity) = size?(which?(bag,equal-self?,entity))

Set's methods synthesis

Exactly following its specification, we can build set's add by calling on container's methods, is-in? and add.

Pair and Relation's methods synthesis

Just as in the C++ implementation, class relation is implemented as a set of pairs. In contrast to that implementation, no pointers are necessary. Thus, we bypass the class element in the definition of class pair (Figure 7)

```
class pair inherit from entity

constructor
pair make-pair(entity,entity1)

queries
entity key?(pair)
entity value?(pair)
pair equal-key?(pair,pair1)
pair equal-value?(pair,pair1)

commands
pair' set-key(pair,entity)
pair' set-value(pair,entity)

Equivalences
(equal(key?(pair), key?(pair1))
            => equal-key?(pair,pair1) = pair
```

(The rest are left as an easy exercise for the reader)

Figure 7. Class pair specification.

As indicated before, all of class pair's methods are considered to be primitives.

The add and remove methods of relation can be easily synthesized from their inherited versions. This leaves remove-all and assoc-all? to synthesize.

Remove-all is obtained by identifying the subset of pairs that match the input key, and telling the included pairs to remove themselves using entity's remove-self[4]:

```
remove-all(relation,key) =
tell-all(which?(relation, equal-key?, key),remove-self, relation)
```

Methods key-is-in? and assoc-all? use a similar approach

```
key-is-in?(relation, key) =
        not (empty? (which?(relation, equal-key?, key))
assoc-all?(relation, key) =
        ask-all (which?(relation, equal-key?, key), value?)
```

---

[4] Defined similarly to add-self.

Function's methods synthesis

Following its specification, class function's add uses the inherited method key-is-in? to prevent adding multiple pairs with the same key. To find the unique value paired with a given key (if it exists) we use which-one? using class pair's equal-key?:

    assoc?(function, key) =
        value?(which-one?(function, equal-key?, key))

Function's replace is just the inherited method remove-all followed by add:

    replace(function,key,value) =
        add(remove-all(function,key),key,value)

List Synthesis

List is synthesized as a subclass of function, the key plays the role of index, while the value is the associated entity. This is the formal version of the parallel implementation of list discussed in Chapter 3. To hold the index, we employ the class number (defined below). Thus,

    list-ref?(list,i) = assoc?(list,number(i))

To insert an entity in position i, we tell all pairs with key greater or equal to increment themselves. Then we use function's add to insert the new pair.

    insert(list,entity,i) = add(tell-all(list, if-greater-inc,i),number(i),entity)

Similarly to remove the entity at position i

    remove(list,i) = tell-all(remove-all(list, number(i)),if-greater-dec,i),

The helping methods, if-greater-inc and if-greater-dec, are easily defined in class number. They are called by methods of the same name from class pair to operate on the key component. The specification of class number is in Figure 8:

```
class number inherit from entity

constructor

number make-number(integer)

queries

integer value?(number)
    bolean equal?(number,number1)

commands

number' set-value(number,integer)
number' if-greater-inc(number,integer)
number' if-greater-dec(number, integer)

Equivalences

(j >= i) => if-greater-inc(number(j),i)
                           = number(j+1)
(j > I) => if-greater-dec(number(j),i) = number(j-1)
```

Figure 8. Class Number Specification.

The synthesis of class order's methods will be addressed in Chapter 10.

9.3 Lessons Learned

This chapter shows that the ensemble methods and a few basic methods are sufficient to implement all the functionality identified in the containers class hierarchy. Since nowhere did we employ knowledge of container's internal structure (it acted as a *private* base class), the construction does not depend on how ensemble methods are implemented. One distinct possibility is to implement the HCCL this way in parallel and distributed computing environments. In such environments, we can exploit the inherent parallelism in the methods to speed up processing. It may certainly be beneficial to build in additional ensemble methods, but we have shown that the ones identified are a set of primitives and therefore a solid place to start.

Problems

1. Define appropriate queries matching the prototype required to apply reduction to compute the maximum of a container of numbers. Simulate the reduction process

for a container of 3 arbitrary numbers. (Hint: let the token be the number with minus infinity as its value.)

Show how to compute the minimum using reduction.

Use tell-all to synthesize the computation of the maximum of a container of numbers.

2. Reduction applies to combination operations on containers such as append, union and intersection. For example, we have already defined append for container. Then the containers in a container can be combined into one following the specification:

container1 append-all(container-of-containers)

is-in?(container-of-containers, container) = T
    and is-in?(container,entity)
        => is-in?(container-of-containers,entity) = T

is-in?(container-of-containers,entity) = F

Specify the union and intersection of a set-of-sets and show how to apply reduction to implement their computation.

3. Synthesize ask-all and which? for a given query using tell-all and a command that is a modified version of the query.

4. Synthesize which-one? using reduce and a modified query:

which-one?(container, query?, args)
    = reduce(container, query-self?, token, args)

Define query-self? which makes this work properly.

5. The ensemble command tell-all(container,command,args) sends the same command and arguments to each object in container. However, it is possible to have each object employ different arguments by sending the complete package of arguments indexed by container objects. The prototype then takes the following form:

tell-all(container, execute-command, fn)

where fn is a function with pairs (obj, args-for-obj). Define the command execute-command that interprets the arriving fn, extracts the proper arguments, and executes the command.

6. Consider a situation where multiple entities are being placed into multiple containers and we want to ask any entity to which containers it belongs. The standard approach would be to keep a container of containers so that an entity can use the which ensemble method to find out those in which it resides. Another approach is to have each entity keep a container to keep track of the containers it is in. In this (latter) case, there is no need for the original containers. They can be replaced by a single container holding all the entities. However, now to find out the contents of a container requires that an appropriate which ensemble method be broadcast to each entity in the "universal" container. Finally, both approaches can be combined (so that there is redundant information being kept). Implement the three alternatives and discuss the advantages and disadvantages of each.

10
Ordered Containers and Their Implementation

We continue with the second branch of the containers specification hierarchy, that of ordered containers (Figure 1). Consideration starts with class order, which is general enough to serve as a base class not only for classes stack, queue, and list, but also for a great many other applications. The underlying new concept is a linear ordering method, called greater-than?, which is assumed to be available to order the items in a container. By characterizing this method as a state-representing query, we obtain a generic capability to order container contents that can be readily specialized to any appropriate subclass. In particular, by properly defining greater-than? for stack, queue, and list, we can derive their behaviors from the base class order. (We will show later in this chapter how this differs from the usual specifications of stacks and queues, which don't take advantage of state-representing queries.)

The last part of the chapter discusses several alternative implementations of the order hierarchy. One approach employs ensemble methods and is therefore appropriate to both parallel and sequential implementation. Given the multiple implementations possible, the choice of which to use must depend on other considerations, such as efficiency.

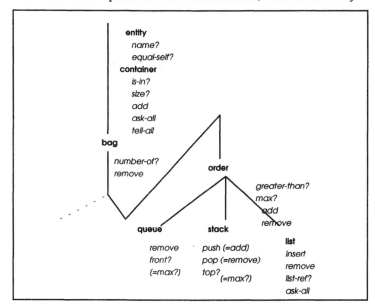

Figure 1. Subhierarchy of ordered containers.

10.1 Class Order

The concept of ordered containers is illustrated in Figure 2. At any time that the container is not empty, we can use max? to ask for the largest item in it. We can add items to the container with the same result as in the base class container, except that add may do more work to help max? do its job. We can also invoke a remove command, which in this case always removes the largest item. This restricted form of removal corresponds to just that required for stack (where it is called pop) and queue. It is not difficult to extend the specification to allow for removal of an arbitrary item.

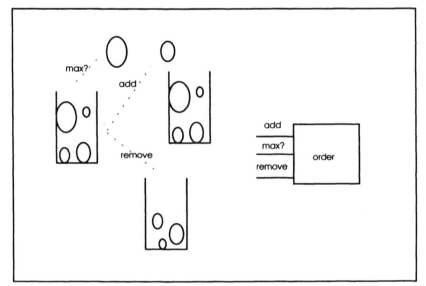

Figure 2. Illustrating class order behavior.

The behavior specification of class order is given in Figure 3:[1]

---

[1] The requirement for linear ordering is omitted from the specification for simplicity. It assures that there is essentially only one maximum for any subcollection of items in the container.

order(entity)   inherits from   *bag*

constructor

make- *order* ()

queries

entity max?(*order*)

Virtual ,hidden

boolean greater-than?(*order, entity1, entity2*)

commands

order' add(*order* , *entity*)
order' remove(*order*)

Domain Restrictions

max?(*order*) = defined provided that empty?(*order*) = F
remove(*order*) = defined provided that empty?(*order*) = F
greater-than?(order, entity1, entity2) = defined
        provided that is-in?(order, entityi) = T, i = 1,2

Equivalences

number-of?(remove(order),max?(order)) =
        number-of?(order,max?(order)) - 1

//the usual axioms defining an   *ordering*   relation:
//*asymmetry:*
    greater-than?(order,entity1,entity2) = T
        => greater-than?(order,entity2,entity1) = F

//transitivity:
greater-than?(order,entity1,entity2) = T
        greater-than?(order,entity2,entity3) = T
            => greater-than?(order,entity1,entity3) = F

// adding or removing an entity
// has no effect on relations among other entities:

greater-than?(add(order,entity), entity2,entity2)
            greater-than?(order, entity1, entity2)

greater-than?(remove(order), entity1,entity2) =
            greater-than?(order, entity1, entity2)

// the following express the properties of the maximum:

size?(order) = 1and is-in?(order,entity) = T
            => max?(order)= entity

is-in?(order,entity) = T and equal(entity,max?(order)) = F
            =>greater-than?(order, max?(order),entity)

Figure 3. Object behavior specification of class order.

Having probably run across discussions of sorting algorithms before, you may be wondering why sorting is not mentioned explicitly in the specification. The reason is that class order characterizes the most basic behavior required for sorting. Indeed, successively removing the maximum from an order instance generates a sorted sequence of its objects. However, there are many uses of class order where we are not interested in a complete sort of items but rather only in the maximum. For example, if you are considering several cars to buy, then you are interested in finding the best one for your needs, not in ranking them all.

Implementation Preliminaries

Let's first consider a special case of the implementation of the order class in the form of a subclass containing only numerical items. In this implementation, we will keep only a single instance variable – for the maximum so far observed. We assume that the class number, a derived class of entity, has been correctly implemented as specified in Chapter 9.

```
class num_order:public bag{
private:
number * maximum;
public:
void add(number *n);
number * n get_max();
void remove();
};
```

Further, to implement the updating of the maximum performed by the add command, a newly added number that exceeds the existing maximum replaces it:

```
void num_order::add(number * n){
if (maximum == NULL | |
  n->get_value() > maximum->get_value()))
maximum = n;
}
```

The query for maximum merely reads the updated maximum:

```
number * num_order::get_max(){
return maximum;
}
```

Note that this stripped down version of order having only methods, add, greater-than? and max? is all we need for finding the best of a given collection of alternatives. The problem comes when we include remove. When the maximum is removed, the next greatest item needs to be computed. Since there can be any number of removes (of course, less than the number of items), it won't suffice to keep track of just the previous maximum.

One simple solution is to employ bag's add and remove to maintain the correct state of the container:

```
void num_order::add(number * n){
if (maximum == NULL | |
  n->get_value() > maximum->get_value()))
  maximum = n;
bag::add(n);
}

void num_order::remove(){
bag::remove(maximum );
 compute_max();
}
```

Here compute_max scans through all items in the bag and selects the maximum. One way to do this takes advantage of the comparison already performed in order's add:

```
void compute_max(){
num_order * temp = new num_order();
tellall1(this, number, add_self,temp);
maximum = temp->get_max();
}
```

Explanation: the new maximum will emerge after the end of adding all the numbers to the temporary num_order instance. Note that this is a reduction implemented with the tellall ensemble method.

The implementation just given requires a complete scan of all items each time the maximum needs to be recomputed. This can be very time consuming for large containers. Many other implementations are possible. Typically they create an explicit representation of the greater-than? relation and use this to retrieve the maximum in one step. The cost for this benefit is that a newly added entity must be inserted in the right place in the explicit representation on each insertion. However, this process does not necessarily have to traverse all the items. In the simplest approach, discussed at the end of this Chapter, only half the items have to be traversed on the average. Sorting algorithms such as bubble sort and quick sort do even less traversal. In the case of stacks and the queues, we will see that the insertion point is known in advance and the result is similar to the usual linked list implementations of these behaviors (see the Problems).

Recall however, that many applications of order require only computing a best alternative. In such cases, the work required to place items in sorted order would not be justified.

Generic Implementation

We develop a generic implementation of class order by generalizing the specific approach just discussed:

```
class order:public bag{
protected:
entity * maximum;
public:
void add(entity *n);
entity * n get_max();
void remove();
virtual Bool greater_than(entity *n, entity *m);
};
```

The greater_than relation is virtual for order and supplied by the specific derived class order under consideration. For example, with number is derived from entity, then we declare:

```
class num_order: public order{
Bool greater_than(number *n, number *m){
return ((number *)n->get_value() >
    ((number *)m->get_value()));
}
```

The relationship between abstract and concrete classes is shown in Figure 4.

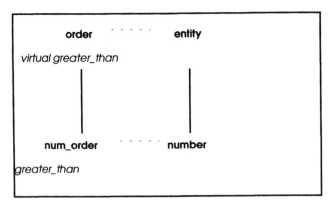

Figure 4. Abstract and concrete classes for ordering.

Now the rest of the definitions are (mostly) straightforward:

```
void order::add(entity * n){
(if (maximum == NULL | | greater_than(n,maximum))
   maximum = n;
bag::add(n)
}

entity * order::get_max(){
return maximum;
}

void order::remove(){
bag::remove(maximum );
 compute_max();
}
```

For compute_max we would like to use similar text to that above. But it turns out that
this will not allow the proper bindings to work when order and entity are replaced by their
concrete derived class counterparts. This would mean that we would have to rewrite
compute_max in every such concrete class. However, there is an approach that does
allow the bindings to be made properly. This is done using the copy macro:

```
void order::compute_max(){
container * r = new container();
copy_to(r);
copy_back(r);
}

void order::copy_to(container * r){
copy(this, entity,r);
}

void order::copy_back(container * r){
maximum = NULL;
head = NULL;
length = 0;
copy(r, entity,this);
}
```

Note that we copy the elements into a temporary container, then clear, and add them back.
This works because the latter add operation employs the method of the **current** derived
subclass of order, thereby invoking the right version of greater_than to order the entries.

10.2 Stacks and Queues

We can easily formulate the appropriate greater_than relation for classes stack and queue. The ordering for these classes will be based on a sequence number. For stack, the most recently added entity will have the higher sequence number and will be ranked highest. Since we always look at and remove the highest ranked item, this gives the required last-in/-first-out (LIFO) behavior. For queue, the ranking is exactly the opposite – the lower the sequence number the higher the ranking. This gives rise to first-in/first-out (FIFO) behavior because the highest ranked item (with the lowest sequence number) has been waiting the longest in the queue.

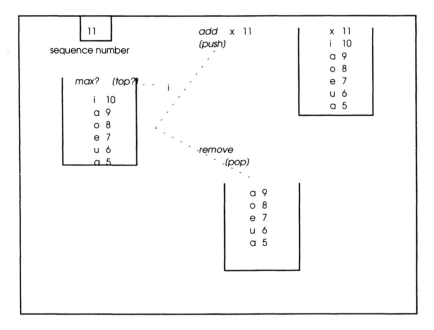

Figure 5. Class stack as a derived class of order.

The formulation of stack and queue as subclasses of order is illustrated in Figure 5 and Figure 6, respectively. Note that there may be several occurrences of the same object. For example, a appears twice, with different order positions. A model of a stack is a physical pile of trays. A new item (tray) is pushed on top of the stack. The tray removed from, or popped off, the stack is the one that has been most recently pushed on to it. Think of the sequence number as the ticket that some stores, post offices, or vehicle registration bureaus, require you to take upon entering.

A model for a queue is a line of cars waiting at a red light (or indeed, any line of customers waiting for service). A new item (car) is added to the end of the line. Items (cars) leave the line in the order of arrival since they are removed from the front of the line. Note that sequence numbers (tickets) are used to relieve customers of having to stand in, or form, a physical waiting line. Usually the lowest numbered customer is the one next served (removed) – just as in our queue implementation.

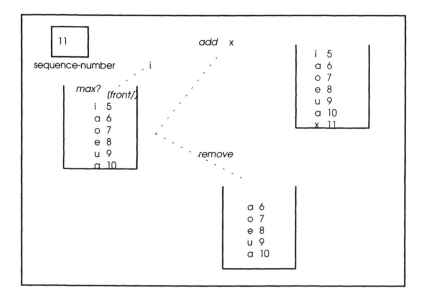

Figure 6. Class queue as a derived class of Order.

To implement classes stack and queue, we define them as subclasses of order:

```
class stack:public order{
private:
number seq_num;
...
}

class queue:public order
{
private:
number seq_num;
...
}
```

We employ the class number for sequence numbering capability and combine it with the subclass of entity for items that will be stacked or queued. If only a name is needed, we can use number itself. We then define the greater_than method for stack to be directly based on highest sequence number:

```
Bool stack::greater_than(number *n, number *m){
```

```
return n->greater_than(m);
}
```

Conversely, the greater-than method for queues ranks low sequence number over high sequence number:

```
Bool queue::greater_than(number *n, number *m){
return m->greater_than(n);
}
```

The rest is just to rename the methods of stacks and queues to their more common forms:

```
stack::push(char *nm){
seq_num++;
add(new number(nm,seq_num));
}

stack::pop(){
remove()
}

stack::top(){
return get_max():
}

queue::add(char *nm){
seq_num++;
bag::add(new number(nm,seq_num));
}


queue::front(){
return get_max();
}
```

Object Behavior Specifications: Stack and Queue

Although we implemented classes stack and queue, we did not provide the required object behavior specifications for them. This just requires that we provide the specific form of the linear order, greater-than?, that enables max? to select the proper item in the container. The right forms of the linear order to use are suggested by the role of the sequence-number in the above implementation. Indeed, in a stack, the most recent addition outranks all included items; in a queue, the most recent addition ranks below all other items in the container. This suggests the following specifications

stack inherits from *order*
//specify greater-than? ordering
//a,b,c,x are entities

greater-than?(add(*order*,a),a,x) = T
        //just added *entity* ranks *higher*
        //than those already present

greater-than?(add(*order*,a),b,c)
    = greater-than?(*order*,b,c)

and

queue inherit from *order*

greater-than?(add(*order*,a),a,x) = F
//just added *entity* ranks *below*
//those already present
greater-than?(add(*order*,a),b,c)
    = greater-than?(*order*,b,c)

With these specific orderings, stack and queue specifications can be shown to satisfy the traditional axioms of stack and queue (Problem 3).

10.3 List as a Subclass of Order

Recall that list behavior was specified directly in Chapter 3. However, a list can be viewed more systematically as an ordered container and hence as a subclass of order. The greater-than? ordering in this case is based on the positions of items in the list. The beginning of the list can be taken as the largest item, with each successive position being ranked lower. Full details are worked out in the Problems.

    Although we have specified list as a subclass of order, it may be more efficient to *implement* the classes in the *reverse* order. Once more, please note the distinction between specification and implementation: we can specify the behavior of a class one way and implement this behavior in yet another. This approach will be discussed next when we consider a list-based implementation of class order.

Implementing Order Classes with List and Ensemble Methods

Earlier in the chapter, we have saw how class order can be implemented with ensemble methods. However, that implementation used copying back and forth, an inefficient approach. We will now employ ensemble methods to derive class order from class list in a manner that avoids copying. Recall that we saw how ensemble methods can synthesize list behavior in Chapter 9. To implement an order we will let the list hold items in descending order according to the greater-than? relation of order. Thus the max? query is implemented by calling list-ref? with argument 0. Likewise, order's remove command is implemented by list's removal of the 0th item. Now, in this approach, order's add command must find the right position to insert its entity argument. Either the new entity is a new maximum, in which case it must be inserted in the 0th position, or else the incoming entity must be inserted at the <u>smallest</u> index whose associated entity is greater than it. The latter search can be done by a reduction, which is the last of the ensemble methods.

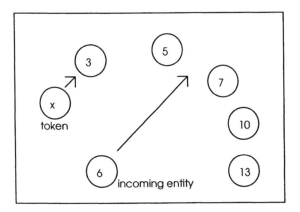

Figure 7. Illustrating reduction to find the insertion point.

In Figure 7 the incoming entity with value 6 should be placed into the slot between the 5 and the 7. Imagine a token that circulates among the items (not necessarily in any fixed order) and checks whether the item lies between 6 and its current value; if so, it takes the place of the current value in the token. Items less than 6 can't satisfy this criterion. Among those greater than 6, the 7 is the smallest and therefore will be the final token value independently of the scanning order. Thus, the 6 must be inserted just before the 7.

As discussed earlier, classes stack and queue were specified as derived from class order. Also, we have seen that they can be implemented directly from class list. Using the approach just taken for order, it is not hard to see how stack and queue can be implemented with ensemble methods (see the Problems).

Problems

1. Extend the specification of class order to include removal of an arbitrary entity, as in bag. Implement this removal command for all the implementations given in the text.

2.(a) Implement class order using ensemble methods with a more straightforward approach than given in the text. (Hint: use reduce to implement compute-max.)

(b) Implement classes stack and queue using ensemble methods.

3. Traditional abstract data type (ADT) specifications of stack and queue employ the following equivalences:

stack

max?(add(order,entity)) = entity
remove(add(order,entity)) = order

queue

max?(add(order,entity)) = max?(order)
size(order) > 0 =>
  remove(add(order,entity)) = add(remove(order),entity)
remove(add(order,entity)) = order

Use the equations for the stack and queue behavior (in the text) to prove that stack and queue satisfy these axioms.

Although the traditional specifications happen to be simpler in the case of stack and queue, this is somewhat of an accident. Since ADTs do not recognize the concept of state-representing queries, they do not support a straightforward specification methodology. For example, try to express the list object behavior in ADT format.
4. Specify list behavior as a subclass of order (see the Appendix for the answer).
5. Some of the ensemble methods must be specialized for class list so as to preserve the order in which the elements are found. The specifications for tell-all and ask-all for list are:

list′ tell-all(list,command,args)

size?(tell-all(list,command,args),i)= size?(list)

list-ref?(tell-all(list,command,args),i)

  = command(list-ref?(list,i), args)

list1 ask-all(list,query,args)

size?(ask-all(list,query, args),i) = size?(list)

list-ref?(ask-all(list,query ,args),i)

  = query(list-ref?(list,i) , args)

Write macros analogous to those in the appendix of Chapter 6 to implement these ensemble methods for list.

Write specifications for the ensemble methods which?, which-one? and reduce. Write macros to implement these methods in C++.

Appendix: Specifying list as a subclass of order

list inherits from *order*

queries

entity list-ref?(list,i)
number length?(list)

commands

list' insert(list,i,entity)
list' remove(list,i)

Equivalences

length?(list) = size?(list)

list-ref?(list,i) = max?($remove^i$(list))

where $remove^0$(list)=list
and $remove^{i+1}$(list)= remove($remove^i$(list))

(remove refers to the remove command inherited from order which removes the max?; $remove^i$(list) removes the i highest items in the container)

Specify the effect of insert on greater-than? as follows:

Let entity_i = list-ref?(list,i) , entity_j = list-ref?(list,j).

k < i =>
greater-than?(insert(list,entity,k),entity,entity_i,) = F

i < k < j =>
greater-than?(insert(list,entity,k),entity,entity_i) = T
and
greater-than?(insert(list,entity,k),entity ,entity_j) = F

k > j =>
greater-than?(insert(list,entity,k),entity,entity_j) = T

greater-than?(insert(list,entity,i),entity_i,entity_j)
   = greater-than?(list,entity_i,entity_j)

The effect of removal is not to disturb the order of items still in the container:

greaterthan?(remove(list,k),entity_i,entity_j)
  = greater-than?(list,entity_i,entity_j)

(Domain restrictions are the same as in the direct specification given earlier.)

11
More Useful Concepts for Containers

This chapter starts by showing how predicate logic constructs, such as ∀ (for all) and ∃ (there exists), can be formulated as ensemble methods for containers. Such methods are not really new since they can be derived from those already discussed. However, for efficiency reasons, it may be desirable to implement them as primitives in an OOP environment.

We then discuss the problem of defining *equality* for the different container classes. The approach we adopted earlier, of using state-representing queries, helps to formulate the appropriate concepts. This leads to a discussion of general set theory operations. Finally, we show how logic ensemble methods make it straightforward to implement equality and set theory methods.

11.1 Logic Ensemble Methods

We have seen ensemble methods for containers that deal with all items as a group. We claimed that the five we enumerated – *tell-all, ask-all, which?, which-one?*, and *reduce* – are primitives so that any other ensemble method can be built up using these methods. Let's now examine some very useful ensemble methods that express the fundamental queries of predicate logic. In such a logical language, we form sentences out of predicates that apply to individuals by applying the quantifiers ∀ and ∃, which mean *for every* and *there exists*, respectively. For example, let $P(x)$ mean "property P is true of individual x." Then $\forall x P(x)$ means that "property P is true of every individual", and $\exists x P(x)$ means that "there is an individual for which property P is true." Another way of expressing that last idea is that that property P is true of some individuals (at least one).

In basic logic, the set of all individuals under consideration is called the universe and is not further divided into subsets. However, if we think of individuals as items in a container, then the extrapolation of the concepts $\forall x P(x)$ and $\exists x P(x)$ is immediate. They become boolean queries that summarize the results of asking all entities in a container a particular boolean query, P.

For example, think of an airplane ready for takeoff. The cabin crew are responsible for checking that all passengers have their seatbelts fastened. If any passenger has a dangling seatbelt, the plane is not allowed to take off. Let's express this using HCCL concepts.

Let the airplane be modeled as a container, p of objects of class passenger. Let this class have a boolean query, seat_belt_fastened?. Then the cabin crew are performing the ensemble method all?(p, seat_belt_fastened?),which returns TRUE only if all the objects in p return TRUE to the query, seat_belt_fastened?. Similarly, let seat_belt_dangling? be the negation of seat_belt_fastened?. Then if some?(p, seat_belt_dangling?) = TRUE, the crew will politely tell the offending passenger(s) to buckle up. Only when all?(p, seat_belt_fastened) = TRUE will the plane be able to take off.

The object behavior specifications of ensemble methods all?, some?, and none? are given in Figure 1.

```
boolean all?(container,query,args)

  all?(container,query,args) ==

    (size?(which?(container,query,args))) = size?(container))

boolean some?(container,query,args)

  some?(container,query,args) ==

            (size?(which?(container))) > 0 )

boolean none?(container,query,args)

  none?(container,query,args) ==

            (not (some?(container,query,args) ))
```

Figure 1. Specification of ensemble logic methods.

Implementation

If our claim is true that tell-all, ask-all, which?, which-one?, and reduce are primitives, then we should be able to synthesize the logic ensemble methods from them. Indeed, the specifications in Figure 1 are stated in terms of ensemble methods. Let's investigate alternative implementations. One way to implement all? in a C++ macro has this form:

```
all(container,query,args){
container * results = new container();
which(container,entity, query,args,results);
return results->size() == container()->size();
}
```

Here we collect the entities that return T to a query in a container and compare its size with the size of the original container. Another possibility is to check which entities return F; we return F if any do:

```
all(container,query,args){
container * results = new container();
which_not(container,entity, query,args,results);
return results->empty();
}
```

A simple transformation of the second implementation gives an implementation of some? :

```
some(container,query,args){
container * results = new container();
which(container,entity, query,args,results);
return !results->empty();
}
```

We said earlier that even though tell-all, ask-all, which?, which-one?, and reduce are primitives, we may want to implement other methods directly for efficiency reasons. For example, we can tell that all? is false as soon as one counterexample has been found. Thus, in a sequential processing environment, we would prefer an implementation of this form:

```
all(container, class, query,args){
for (p = container->get_head(), p!=NULL, p =p>get_right()){
if (!(class *)p->get_ent()->query(args)) return F;
return T;
}
```

Here we stop as soon as one F is obtained, thus reducing computation time.

Example: Room, Doors, Alarms

Let's put alarms on windows and doors of a room. A container, alarms, will hold the instances of the alarm class, discussed earlier. To close the doors and windows and arm the alarms, we use the ensemble method tell-all:

```
tellall(alarms,alarm,close);
tellall(alarms,alarm,arm);
```

To ask if all alarms are armed and ready to do their jobs, we use the logic ensemble method all?:

```
all?(alarms,armed?)
```

To ask if some door or window has been broken into, we use the logic ensemble method, some?:

```
some?( alarms, sounding?)
```

11.2 Container Equality

When are two containers equal? The answer is easy, if by "equality" we mean "identity," that is, containers are equal only if they are really the same object. This is the equality that is implemented in the default method equal in HCCL (see Chapter 6). However, often we want to compare nonidentical containers to see if they are "essentially" the same. What can this mean? Actually, the same considerations hold for every class of objects. Indeed, there are some properties of "equality" in general that constrain the meanings we can give it. Think of triangles in plane geometry. When are two triangles essentially the same? You'll remember the answer: when they are *congruent*, that is , when one can be moved and rotated to fit exactly over the other. More concretely, it turns out that such congruence requires, for example, that the triangles have an equal side and two equal angles. More abstractly, congruence is an *equivalence* relation, having the properties of *reflexivity, symmetry,* and *transitivity.* In general, equality must have these properties.

In the case of containers, no matter how we define the query Equal:[1]

```
boolean Equal(container,container1)
```

we would require that

```
Equal(c1,c1) (reflexivity: identical containers are Equal)
Equal(c1,c2) = T ⇒ Equal(c2,c1) = T (symmetry)
Equal(c1,c2) = T
    and Equal(c2,c3) = T ⇒ Equal(c1,c3) = T (transitivity).
```

---

[1] using the capital E, to distinguish it from the existing *equal* in HCCL

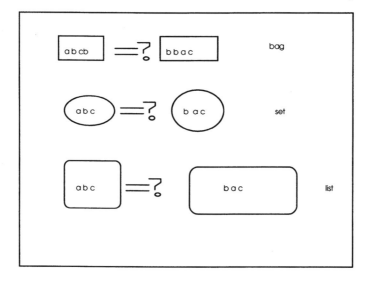

Figure 2. Which pairs are Equal?

Now looking at Figure 2, we have some typical examples of pairs of containers that beg to be judged for equality. Although none of the pairs is identical, we would judge the bags and sets to be Equal, but not the lists. Why?

In the specification of class container, we employed the two state-representing queries: is-in? and size?. Therefore we should consider *two containers to be equal if they can't be distinguished by the state-representing queries.* In other words, two containers are equal if they have been brought to the same state, as far as the state-representing queries are concerned, by their respective construction sequences. The same concept obviously applies to any class of objects.

This leads us to consider two containers to be equal if they have the same size (we can't tell them apart by the size? query) and if they have the same items (we can't tell them apart by the is-in? query).

This can be expressed as

Equal(c1,c2) =
    (size?(c1) = size?(c2)
        and (∀e)(is-in?(c1,e) = T ⟹ is-in?(c2,e) = T))

Notice that we have to use the universal quantifier ∀ to express this definition. (Since we now have its ensemble method equivalent all? at our disposal, we can express the specification using it.) However, to avoid getting too bound up in abstract definitions, we will skip right to an implementation in C++.

```
Bool container::Equal(container *c){
if (size() != c->size())
return F;
```

```
    else
    return all1(this,entity,am_in,c);
    }
```

where

```
    entity::am_in(container *c){
    c->is_in(this);
    }
```

In other words, if the size of an incoming container is not the same as this one, they are not Equal; otherwise (the sizes match and) we ask each entity in our container if it is in the incoming container. If they all respond affirmatively, then we have equality as measured by Equal.

Defining equality in terms of state-representing queries works for all container classes. For example, the state representing queries of class bag are size? and number-of? So the appropriate definition is:

```
Equal(b1,b2) =
    (size?(b1) = size?(b2)
        and every item in b1
        has the same number of occurrences in b2)
```

An implementation using the logic ensemble method all? is

```
Bool bag::Equal(bag * b){
if (size() != b->size())
return F;
else
all2(this,entity,eq_num,this,b);
}
```

where

```
    entity::eq_num(bag * b1,bag * b2){
    return b1->number_of(this) == b2->number_of(this);
    }
```

Equality for classes set and list can be defined in the same manner (see the Problems).

11.3 Inclusion, Union, Intersection, and Difference

Equality in classical set theory is actually one of a few fundamental binary operations. For example, we have the following:

- S ⊆ S' (subset or inclusion: every element in S is a member of S')
- S∪ S' (union: the smallest set that includes both S and S')
- S∩ S' (intersection: the largest set that is included in both S and S')
- S- S' (difference: the largest set that is included in S but not included in S')

Set equality can then be defined as

S = S' if S ⊆ S' and S' ⊆ S,

that is, two sets are equal if each one is a subset of the other.

Indeed, by dropping the requirement that containers have the same size, the definition of Equal becomes the one for inclusion:

```
included_in?(c1,c2) =
  ( ∀e)( is-in?(c1,e) = T => is-in?(c2,e) = T))
```

and this can be implemented in C++ by

```
Bool container:: included_in (container *c){
all1(this,entity,am_in,c);
}
```

The definition and implementation of included_in for classes bag, set and list follow this same pattern (see Problems).

The union, intersection, and difference operations can be similarly implemented with ensemble methods (see the Problems and the Appendix).

11.4 Conversion

In the chain of derived classes: container→bag→set→order, a higher-level class can be converted to a lower-level one. As illustrated in Table 1, when such a conversion is performed, some useful work is accomplished.

Table 1. Work done by conversion from container to subclass.

container	Word done
bag	counts of occurrences
set	identify distinct members
order	sort according to "greater than"

Each of these conversions follows the pattern in the example:

```
bag * container::container_to_bag(){
bag * b = new bag();
copy(this, entity,b);
return b;
}
```

You should remember the work done by conversion for application in many situations. For example, converting a container of text to a bag will provide word frequencies in the text. Converting the bag to a set will identity the words found in the text. Converting this set to the appropriate order subclass will sort the words according to their frequencies of occurrence in the text (see the Problems).

11.5 Container Comparison

The next step beyond judging whether containers are equal is to compare them for insertion them in an order. One simple means of comparing containers employs their sizes. Such a concept of greater-than? can be used to sort a container of containers. Here we would define an appropriate greater-than? method to compare sizes:

```
greater-than?(container,container1)
    = (size?(container) > size?(container1))
```

Notice that any definition of greater-than? has to be compatible with the definition of equality given earlier – if greater-than? returns TRUE then Equal must return FALSE.

More general comparison can be obtained by using reduction on containers and comparing the results. For example, containers of numbers might be reduced to their maximum values with comparison based on these maxima (see the Problems).

For ordered containers, the underlying order itself can play a role in their comparison. For example, two lists of equal length can be compared by comparing their first elements – if these are equal then we go on to compare the second elements, otherwise we return the results as the result of the comparison. This iteration continues to successive elements as needed. *Lexicographical ordering* is the name given to this form of comparison since it corresponds to the ordering of words in a dictionary – shorter words come before longer words and words of equal length are ordered by their first letter, then by their second if necessary, and on (see Problems).

Lexicographical ordering can also be used to order general objects based on their states. For example, let class house have instance variables, location, price, and square-footage. Then home buyers might rank houses by deciding on a priority ordering of these features and then employing a lexicographical principle. For example, with the priority just given, the location of a house is considered first – only if two houses are equally ranked in location would one go on to consider their price and square-footage rankings (see the Problems).

Problems

1. Define the method Equal for classes set and list. (Hint: Equal for set can be inherited from bag; use the state-defining queries get_length and list_ref for list::Equal.)

2. Define the method included_in for classes bag, set and list. (Hint: drop the requirement for equal sizes from the definition of Equal. For list, interpret included_in as sublist, i.e., the first list can be found in the second list, though not necessarily starting from position 0.)

3. As discussed in the text, set theory defines operations on sets such as union, intersection, and difference. Specify these operations in class set and implement them in C++ (answers are in the appendix).

4. Test your implementations based on your specifications using the methodology of Chapter 7.

5. Specify, implement, and test a class String, each instance of which is a list of character entities. String is an object-oriented formulation of the type char * which represents a string as an array of characters. Provide methods for String that correspond to those provided in C++ such as strcpy, strcmp, substr, and strlen. (Hint: define class character as a subclass of entity and derive String from list inheriting its Equal query. Define greater_than for String based on the lexicographical principle discussed in the text.)

6. Write a procedure to print out the String instances in a container in the order of their frequency of occurrences, the most frequent first. (Hint: carry out the conversions discussed in the text.)

7. Write a conversion for each of the cases corresponding to the "x" in the following table:

from↓ to →	container	bag	set	list
container		x	x	x
bag			x	x
set				x
list		x	x	

Give an example of application for each of the checked cases.

8. Consider the following inheritance hierarchy:

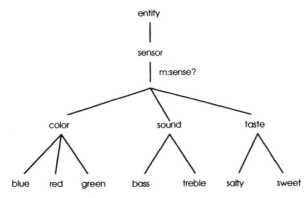

as well as:

Method sensor::sense?(physical_object_instance) returns a container of sensor instances that report TRUE when their methods sense? is applied to physical_object_instance.

In C++ implement the class hierarchy and methods in such a way that the definitions of the methods of all existing classes are not affected when a new subclass of sensor is added. Also take maximum advantage of inheritance in minimizing the amount of code.

Show that to add a new subclass of sensor named tactile, with subclasses soft and hard, none of the previous definitions need be modified to continue to work properly.

9. A region is a set of points. Set-of-regions is a set of regions. A method assign-region decides to which region of set-of-regions a given point belongs. It does so by returning the region whose average of the distances of its points to the given point is the smallest (assume that no ties occur).

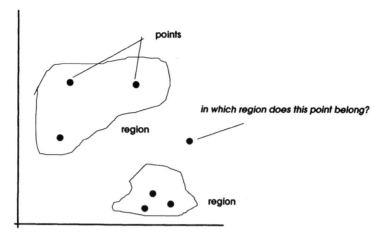

In C++ define the classes for points and regions as well as a subclass of order for ordering regions. Using ensemble methods define the method assign-region for the order subclass.

10. Specify, implement, and test a software system for helping home buyers evaluate houses. Employ the lexicographical principle discussed in the text but in addition, give buyers the flexibility to choose the priority ranking of features to reflects their most important concerns.

Appendix: Specifying and Implementing Set theory Operations

The specifications for union, intersection, and difference are given as well as their implementation in C++ using ensemble methods.

For union the specification is

set2 union(set,set1)

is-in?(union(set,set1),entity) =
      (is-in?(set,entity)) = T
         or is-in?(set1,entity)) = T)

An implementation is

```
set * set::union(set * set1){
set * set2 = new set();
tellall1(this, entity, add_self, set2);
tellall1(set1, entity, add_self, set2);
return set2;
}
```

For intersection the specification is

set2 *intersection*(set,set1)

is-in?(intersection(set,set1),entity) =
    (is-in?(set,entity)) = T
        and is-in?(set1,entity)) = T)

An implementation is

```
set * set::intersection(set * set1){
set * set2 = new set();
tellall2(this, entity, if_in_add_self, set1,set2);
return set2;
}
```

where if_in_add_self(set1,set2) adds an entity to set2 only if it is in set1.

For difference the specification is

set2 *difference*(set,set1)

is-in?(difference(set,set1),entity) =
    (is-in?(set,entity)) = T
        and is-in?(set1,entity)) = F)

An implementation is:

```
set2 * set::difference(set * set1){
set * set2 = new set();
tellall2(this, entity, if_not_in_add_self, set1,set2);
return set2;
}
```

12
Design Based on Hierarchical Decomposition and Ensemble Methods

This chapter presents a variety of examples of fairly complex systems that can be given quite elegant constructions using the concepts developed in the previous chapters. The key concept is to decompose a system in a top down manner so that a hierarchically constructed container is obtained. This enables the required behavior to be implemented with ensemble methods at each level.

12.1 Trees as Hierarchical Containers

We start with the specification and implementation of tree structures. These classical data structures can be viewed as hierarchical containers, as illustrated in Figure 1. Viewing trees as hierarchical containers enables us to apply container methods and especially the ensemble methods for sequential and parallel computation. Each *node* is either a leaf or a container of lower level nodes, called its *children*. The *root* is the only node not in a such a container. In Figure 1, node *a* is the root and has children *b,c,* and *d*. The leaves are *b,e,f,* and *d*. A tree does not permit cyclic paths. For example, node *c* cannot be added as a child of node *f* lest it become its own ancestor. However, checking for such cyclic paths is time consuming. Often, one can avoid such checking by ensuring that only new entities are added to the tree.

Different types of containers can be used to hold children of nodes. The class set would be appropriate where we want to maintain only distinct entities as siblings. The class bag allows multiple copies of entities. An ordered container, such as a list, keeps siblings in a specified order, which is useful for evaluating expressions.

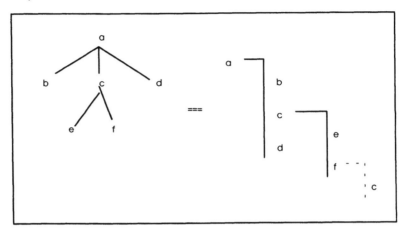

Figure 1. Representing a tree as a container of containers.

A tree class can be specified as a subclass of container. Actually, a tree is a kind of ordered container where the contents, or nodes, are ordered by a parent-child relationship. The most straightforward specification, given in Figure 2, allows adding only new entities (not already in the tree, so an entity occurs at most once). In this case sets can be used as the containers. The specification does not assume that such a tree is actually implemented as a set of sets, although that would be one possible implementation for it.

tree(entity)

constructor

tree make-tree(entity) //entity will be the root

queries

entity root?(tree)
boolean leaf?(tree, entity)
boolean node?(tree,entity)
boolean child?(tree,entity,entity1)

command

tree' add(tree,parent,child) // parent and child are entities

Domain Restrictions

add(tree,parent,child) = defined
                    provided that node?(tree, child) = F

child?(tree, parent,child) = defined
                    provided that leaf?(tree, parent) = F

Equivalences

root?(make-tree(root)) = root
root?(add(tree,parent,child),child)) = root

leaf?(make-tree(root),root) = T
leaf?(add(tree,parent,child),child) = T
leaf?(add(tree,parent,child),parent) =F
leaf?(add(tree,parent,child),entity) = leaf?(tree,entity)

node?(make-tree(root),root) = T
node?(make-tree(root),entity) = F
node?(add(tree,parent,child),child) = T
node?(add(tree,parent,child),entity) = node?(tree,entity)

child?(make-tree(root),parent,child) = F
child?(add(tree,parent,child),parent,child) =T
child?(add(tree,parent,child),entity,entity1)
                    = child?(tree, parent,child)

Figure 2. Specification of class tree.

If we allow multiple instances of entities as nodes in a tree, there is a danger that an entity will be added under one parent that is already a child of another. To disallow multiple parentage in a tree, we can restrict the add command appropriately (see the Problems).

Since single parentage is very restrictive, we can allow multiple parentage but take precautions to prevent cycles from occurring. This requires us to keep track of the ancestry of nodes. Let's examine how ancestor? is specified.

When the tree is constructed, there are no pairs related by ancestry:

ancestor?(make-tree(root), grandparent, child) = F

When we add a child beneath a parent, the parent becomes an ancestor of the child:

ancestor?(add(tree, parent, child),parent, child) = T

But also any ancestor of the parent becomes an ancestor of the child as well:

ancestor?(tree,grandparent,parent) = T

⇒ ancestor?(add(tree, parent,child),grandparent, child)

The relationship of any other pairs of nodes is not affected by this particular addition:

ancestor?(add(tree, parent, child),entity1,entity2)

= ancestor?(tree, entity1, entity2)

In this multiple occurrence specification, we did not impose any restriction on the children that could be added to a parent. Thus, the generic class container can be used to hold these children. Adding such restrictions might determine the appropriate type of container. For example, we could add a query eldest? that returns the earliest child added to a parent. Indeed we could ask for the children of a parent in the order of age (order in which they were added). Then a queue would be the appropriate container for children.

Using the HCCL, implementation of trees is straightforward (see the Problems).

12.2 Tree Computations with Ensemble Methods

Tree structures are often used in computations. They might be constructed during an *analysis* phase (top down) that is later followed by a *synthesis* phase that starts from the leaves (bottom up). Both the top-down and bottom-up processing can exploit parallelism. In the top-down phase, as the tree fans out, individual computations and construction of children can be performed in parallel within *echelons* (all nodes at the same level; see the Problems). The reverse wave of computation starts from the bottom up, when the leaves begin their computations. As nodes complete their computations, they send the results to their parents. A parent waits for all of its children's results before proceeding with its own. Once again, computations by nodes in the same echelon are parallelizable. Using this approach, the basic ensemble methods of containers can be implemented in a parallel environment (see the Problems). Since, as will be discussed in Chapter 13, the Java language supports multithreading, it offers a medium for such parallelization.

The use of tree structures and computations just discussed is exemplified in object-oriented parsing and evaluation of expressions. An incoming nested expression can be parsed and mapped into a tree whose nodes represent the operators invoked in the expression. To preserve the order of the arguments in an operator, the list class can be used. The expression can then be evaluated by having each node work on the results of its children's evaluations (see the Problems).

12.3 A Class of Graphics Puzzles

A framework for graphics puzzles is given by the class hierarchy in Figure 3. Three kinds of objects are distinguished, as illustrated in Figure 4:

- *movable visible figures,* shown crosshatched, are the eyes, ears, nose, and mouth in the face puzzle. They can be dragged by the pointer (arrow) and have to be placed within the correct, fixed, invisible figure.
- *fixed invisible figures,* shown with dash-dotted boundary lines, form the invisible zones within which one or more appropriate visible figures must be placed.
- *fixed visible figures,* shown with solid lines (e.g., the face outline), provide the cues that give structure to the puzzle and enable it to be solved.

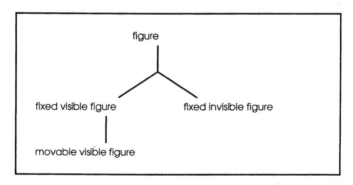

Figure 3. Class hierarchy for the face puzzle.

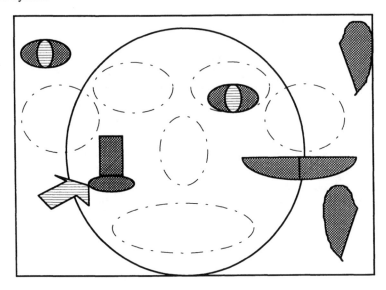

Figure 4. Illustrating the face puzzle.

Figure 6 illustrates a solution to the puzzle characterized by the fact that all movable, visible figures have been placed within the allowed invisible areas.

Figure 5. A solution to the face puzzle.

Our approach to specifying this fairly complex behavior is first to decide on what state information will be needed for the user actions and system responses to work as intended. After some experimentation, we come up with the informal description in Figure 6. The acceptance zones mentioned in the description are illustrated in Figure 7.

state: location of the pointer
attachment status of the pointer
location of each movable visible figure
acceptance status of each movable visible figure (initially unaccepted)
location of each of the fixed invisible figures
            (unchanged after initialization)
location of each of the fixed visible figures (unchanged after
initialization)

actions: move the pointer
press the pointer
release the pointer

responses: cheer when a movable visible figure is accepted
jeer when a movable visible figure is deposited
            in the wrong acceptance zone
terminate when all the movable visible figures are accepted

The effect of the actions on the state is:

move the pointer: affects the location of the pointer and the location
            of the attached movable visible figure, if any

press the pointer: affects the attachment status of the pointer,
            if its location is within a movable visible figure

release the pointer: affects the acceptance status of the attached movable visible
figure (if any) if within the correct acceptance zone, while
            responding cheer; otherwise no change in state and
response
        is jeer; also terminates when no unaccepted movable visible
figures remain.

Figure 6. Informal description of face puzzle.

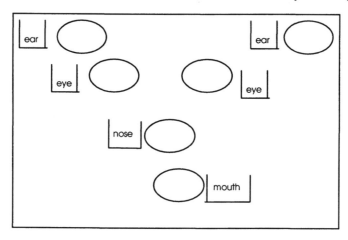

Figure 7. Acceptance zones and associated acceptance sets for face puzzle.

These informal concepts form the basis of a specification which we encourage the reader to attempt (check your results with the specification in the appendix to this chapter).

An implementation can be built around the methods for a pointer class that can be easily synthesized from ensemble methods. A pointer object's first task is to identify which of the movable figure zones contains its current location. After defining a method, is-within?, that checks whether a point lies within the zone of an object, we can implement the pick method for pointer using the ensemble method which-one?:

    pointer::pick

    attached = which-one?(movables, is-within?, location)

The pointer then drags the attached object to a new location where the user thinks that the object can be dropped. The drop method can be described as follows:

    pointer::drop

    invisible = which-one?(invisibles,is-within?,location)

    if(is-in?(acceptable?(invisble), attached)

      then accept(invisible)

In other words, the invisible object whose zone (if any) contains the pointer location is identified using which-one?. We then test whether the attached object is in the acceptable container of objects defined by this invisible zone. If so, we remove the object from the acceptable container and fix its location, i.e., it is moved from the movables to the fixed visibles class.

12.4 General Approach to OO Software Development

This example illustrates a general approach to developing object-oriented software for complex processing tasks.

1. The first step is to analyze the task using state representing query and command concepts and describe it an easily understood, informal manner. The aim of this step is to clarify what the state is, how it is transformed by actions (inputs) and how responses are generated.
2. An object behavior specification is then developed based on this informal description and employs ensemble methods as needed. When the underlying structure is hierarchical, the methods can be developed in a top-down fashion (see next example).
3. The specification is then implemented. The HCCL realization in C++, Java or other languages, is especially convenient in that it enables the powerful ensemble methods of containers to be directly applied. However, even if an object-oriented language does not support generic ensemble methods, their behaviors can still be implemented in lower- level code.

Of course, comprehensive *testing* is required to ensure that the implementation works as intended. Following the methodology introduced in Chapter 7, the development of the test plan should be done after the specification is ready in step 2. Then the test suite should be ready by the time the specification is implemented.

12.5 Alarming a Building

The final example in this chapter will illustrate the use of containers and ensemble methods in a more complex example. Consider installing alarms in a house to prevent break-ins. We want to put alarms on all exterior doors so that when a break-in occurs, appropriate action will be taken. What should this action be? We will first require that the rooms that have been entered be sealed off. But also, to be doubly safe, we want to seal off the rooms that are adjacent to those rooms. By an adjacent room, we mean one that can be entered by an interior door connecting to the room in question.

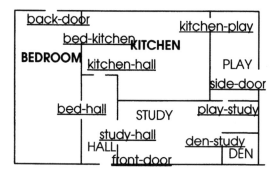

Figure 8. Floor plan of example house.

Based on the floor plan of Figure 8, let's make a catalog of all interior doors and exterior doors in the house. Interior doors are repeated at least twice, under each of the rooms they connect (Figure 9).

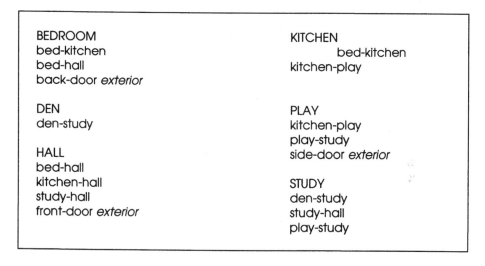

Figure 9. Cataloguing all doors under rooms.

Our task now is to define classes that enable a computer to respond to an alarm by sealing off the room in which the alarm sounded as well as its adjacent rooms. In the hierarchy of classes shown in Figure 10, the class house has an instance variable rooms-in-house and the class room has two instance variables, ext-doors and int-doors, one for each class of door. These instance variables are containers — indeed, they are best made to be sets, because a door is listed at most once under a room (although it must be listed in the catalog twice if it connects between two rooms). We

distinguish the two classes of doors, because exterior doors have alarms with associated
behavior that interior doors do not.

Recall that we required that, when an alarm goes off in a room, the adjacent rooms
are also sealed off. Thus, each room has to have knowledge of its adjacent rooms. But
this knowledge is not independent from the cataloging of doors under rooms — indeed,
it can be computed from that information. Thus, we give each room an instance variable, adjacent-rooms. A house method will compute which rooms are to be included
in this container. This method can be an **intialization** method, which means that it will
be called right after the house has been constructed (i.e., when all the information is
available), and before invoking any of the operational methods.

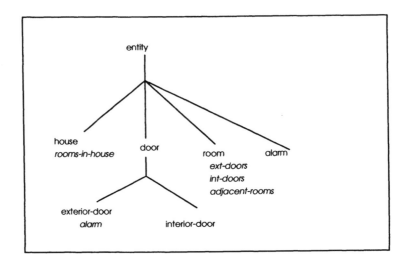

Figure 10. Class hierarchy showing essential instance variables.

Since a house has a hierarchical structure, we can take a top-down approach to defining
constructors:
- make-house(container-of-rooms) creates an instance of a house with rooms-
  in-house := container-of-rooms.
- make-room(exterior doors,interior doors) creates an instance of a room with
  containers:
  - ext-doors := exterior doors,
  - int-doors := interior doors.
- make-int-door creates an interior door.
- make-ext-door creates an exterior door equipped with an alarm.

Although defined top-down, constructors are used to build a house from the bottom
up. We can, for example, construct the house in Figure 8 by creating room instances for

each of the six rooms, adding them to a container, and calling the constructor, make-house . Similarly, we create appropriate interior-door and exterior-door instances for each room instance and then add them to its int-doors and ext-doors using make-room. This gives us enough information for the method compute-adjacent-rooms to work properly.

Once more, progressing from the top downward, a house will tell-all its rooms to compute-adjacent-rooms:

house::compute-adjacent-rooms():

tell-all(rooms-in-house, compute-adjacent-rooms, rooms-in-house)

For a room to be able to compute its adjacent rooms, it must find all the rooms that share a common int-door with it:

room::compute-adjacent-rooms(container-of-rooms):

adjacent-rooms

= which?(container-of-rooms, have-door-in?, int-doors)

The boolean query have-door-in?(doors) checks whether a room has an interior-door in common with doors:

room:: have-door-in?(doors):

!empty?(intersection (doors, int-doors))

(The intersection of two sets was discussed in Chapter 11.)

Having computed adjacent-rooms for each room, we can call upon the ensemble methods, including the logical ensemble methods of Chapter 11, to express the required behavior of the system. For example, starting at the top:

house::close&arm-all-ext-doors():

tell-all(rooms-in-house, close&arm-all-ext-doors)

room::close&arm-all-ext-doors():

tell-all(ext-doors, close&arm)

To express the break-in detection behavior:

house::detect&respond():

house::seal-rooms(house::which-rooms-broken-into?)

house::which-rooms-broken-into?():

which?(rooms-in-house, broken-into?)

room::broken-into?():

some?(ext-doors, alarm-sounding?)

To seal off the rooms in a container and their nearest neighbors:

house::seal-rooms(container):

tell-all(container, seal-room&adjacent-rooms)

room::seal-room&adjacent-rooms():

room::seal-room[1]

tell-all(adjacent-rooms, seal-room)

room:: seal-room():

tell-all (union(ext-doors, int-doors),close)

To test such a design we must set a house instance into an appropriate state before applying a query-terminated sequence of commands. For example, to test which-rooms-broken-into?, we might trip the alarm in the back-door instance made initially. We then test if which-rooms-broken-into? returns the bedroom instance that it should.

12.6 Summary

We have suggested a general approach to developing software for complex tasks based on the containers class hierarchy and its associated ensemble methods. Generally, such tasks require hierarchical compositions in which containers can be components of other containers. Information flow between levels in the hierarchy can be expressed with ensemble methods. Moreover, the hierarchical structure supports top down design of methods and constructors. Implementation of such designs is facilitated by the hierarchical containers with ensemble methods applied at the various levels. As suggested in the Problems, efficient realization of the ensemble methods in parallel environments enables exploitation of multiprocessor architectures to obtain high-speed responses.

Problems

1.
   (a) Implement, and test, the acyclic tree class specified in the text using the C++ class declarations:

---

[1] Actually, this line is not needed; Since a room has doors in common with its own doors, it will always be included in its adjacent rooms.

```
class node: public entity{
protected:

container * children;

... //add in the additional methods

};
```

```
class tree: public container{

protected:

node * root;

container * leaves;

relation * ancestors;

public:

node * get_root();

Bool is_leaf(node *);

Bool is_node(node *);

... //add in the additional methods

};
```

Note that since class container is the base class, its add, is_in, and get_size can be reused in tree. To test whether a named entity can be added as a leaf, a search of ancestors must be done for this name. Use ensemble methods to create ancestors and perform the search.

Develop a *test suite* following the methodology in Chapter 7 based on the specification and the tree class interface declaration *before* you write the implementation of the methods.

(b) Enhance the previous implementation so that a node has an instance variable to keep track of its parent. Redefine the method for searching for ancestors in this new implementation. Discuss the tradeoff between time and memory exhibited in these implementations. Employ the *same* test suite of Problem 1(a) to test the enhanced implementation.

2. Write a specification that restricts children to single parentage but still allows multiple occurrences of the same entity within sibling containers. Implement this specification by employing the parent instance variable in 1(b).

3. Implement and test the following methods in the class tree:

number level?(tree,node)

//tells how far down the tree a node is

level?(make-tree(root),root) = 0

level?(add(tree,parent,child),child) = level?(tree,parent) + 1

level?(add(tree,parent,child),node) = level?(tree,node)

number depth?(tree)// this is the maximum level

depth?(make-tree(root)) = 0

depth?(tree) = level?(tree,parent) $\Rightarrow$

 depth?(add(tree,parent,child)) = depth?(tree) + 1

depth?(add(tree,parent,child)) = depth?(tree)

number identifier?(tree,node)

//gives a unique number to each node in a binary tree

identifier?(tree,root) = 0

identifier?(add(tree,parent,child1,child2), child1)

     = 2*identifier?(tree,parent) + 1

identifier?(add(tree,parent,child1,child2), child2)

     = 2*identifier?(tree,parent) + 2

identifier?(add(tree,parent,child1,child2), entity)

     = identifier?(tree,entity)

(Nodes with identifiers between $2^{lev}-1$ and $2^{lev}+1$ are found at level lev in the tree.)

Test your implementation with tests developed from the specification.

4. Using your tree class definition as a prototype, implement object-oriented expression evaluation in C++. As an example, consider logical expressions built up as in the following example:

    AND * and1 = new AND("and1");

```
AND * and2 = new AND("and2");

OR * or = new OR("or");

NOT * not = new NOT("not");

logic * a = new logic("a",TRUE);

logic * b = new logic("b",FALSE);


and1->insert(a,0);

and1->insert(or,1);

and1->insert(b,2);

or->insert(not,0);

not->insert(a);

or->insert(and2,1)

and2->insert(b,0);

and2->insert(a,1);

and1->print(); //prints the expression "and1(a or(not(a) and2(b a)))"

cout << and1->evaluate(); //prints "0" (for FALSE)
```

The implementation should also support extensibility; namely, any new operator should be able to be incorporated as in the following:

```
class NEWOP: public OP{

public:

Bool evaluate(){

...

// a computation based on evaluating the arguments.

// For example, the computation for AND is:

// return list_ref(0) && list_ref(1);

....

}

};
```

Then newop->print() and newop->evaluate() should work together with existing operators in expressions such as that above. (Hint: define OP as a derived class of list with evaluate as a virtual method. Define AND, OR, and NOT as derived classes of OP, each with their appropriate evaluate methods (use the logic ensemble methods of Chapter 11). Also define logic (which is employed to enter boolean values) as a derived class of OP with its evaluate returning the assigned truth value).

Write a test suite for your implementation before you start implementing.

5. Instead of synthesizing trees manually, they can be constructed by a parsing process. For example, the string expression and(a, or(not(a),and(b a))) should be automatically mapped into the same tree as in Problem 4. Design the parser, exploiting object-orientated extensibility, such that when new operators are added, the parser code is not modified. (Hint: the parser performs a which? scan of a set containing an instance of each operator class looking for the instance whose class name matches the string it is currently examining.)

6. In current massively parallel computers, each processor has an integer identification ranging from 1 to n, the number of processors. Show how to implement the ensemble methods where the command or query arrives to processor 1, which broadcasts it to all the other processors (and, for a query, collects the results). (Hint: use level assignment in Problem 3 to set up a tree of computations discussed in the text (i.e., processor 0 sends to processors 1 and 2 which send to {3,4} and {5,6}, and so on). Also, store parent information in each processor for the reverse flow of query results.)[2]

As an application example, assume that each processor has stored an arbitrary number. Show how a reduction ensemble method can be implemented to compute their maximum.

7. Specify, implement and test the following variations of the face puzzle:

   (a) *diet game:* each of the standard food groups accepts instances of associated types of food. For example, milk goes into the diary food group but not into the vegetable group

   (b) *money change game:* each coin has container for each type of change that can be applied to it. For example, a quarter has a container with two dimes and a nickel, another container for 5 nickels, etc.

8. Design a watering system for lawns. Trees, plants, bushes, flowers, and grass have differing watering needs, and employ different water delivery systems, such as emitters and sprinklers. Further, plants close to certain others, such as cactii, need to have reduced watering. Assume that your highest level class is lawn which has a method which reports the passage of time in fifteen minute intervals.

---

[2] The advantage of the tree-style messaging is that it obviates sending n messages one after the other at processor 1. Instead, each node need only send two messages. A similar distribution of overhead occurs in the reverse flow of results: the receiving bottleneck at processor 1 is replaced by each node receiving two messages from its children and passing on one message to its parent.

Appendix: Specifying a Graphics Puzzle

constructor

puzzle make-puzzle(movable_visibles, fixed_invisibles, acceptance)

   // for simplicity the fixed_visibles are not considered

      // also the initial locations of figures are not given

queries

coordinate pointer-location?(puzzle)
boolean pointer-dragging?(puzzle)
boolean pointer-is-free?(puzzle)
boolean is-attached?(puzzle, entity)
boolean is-accepted?(puzzle,entity)
coordinate entity-location?(puzzle,entity)

hidden
boolean is-movable?(puzzle,entity)
boolean is-invisible?(puzzle,entity)
boolean is-acceptable?(puzzle,entity,entity1)
boolean pointer-within?(puzzle,entity)   //virtual

commands

puzzle' pointer-move(puzzle,coordinate)
puzzle' pick(puzzle)
puzzle' drop(puzzle)

Equivalences

pointer-location?
 (make-puzzle(
   movable_visibles, fixed_invisibles, acceptance))= 0

pointer-dragging?
 (make-puzzle(
   movable_visibles, fixed_invisibles, acceptance)) = F

pointer-is-free?
 (make-puzzle
  (movable_visibles, fixed_invisibles, acceptance)) = T

```
is-attached?
(make-puzzle(movable_visibles,fixed_invisibles,acceptance), entity) = F

is-accepted?
 (make-puzzle(movable_visibles,fixed_invisibles, acceptance),entity) = F

entity-location?
 (make-puzzle
(movable_visibles,fixed_invisibles,acceptance),
     entity) = 0

is-in?(movable visibles,entity) = T =>
 is-movable?
  (make-puzzle
(movable_visibles,fixed_invisibles,acceptance)
     ,entity) =T

is-in?(fixed invisibles,entity) = T =>
    is-invisable?
      (make-puzzle
        (movable_visibles,fixed_invisibles, acceptance),entity) = T

is-in?(acceptance, entity, entity1) =>
 is-acceptable?
  (make-puzzle
   (movable_visibles, fixed invisibles, acceptance)entity,entity1)

// this ends the constructor sections

pointer-location?(pointer-move(puzzle,coordinate))
    = coordinate

is-attached?(puzzle,entity) = T =>
    entity-location?
       (pointer-move(puzzle,coordinate),entity) = coordinate

pointer-is-free?(puzzle) = T
  and pointer-within?(puzzle, entity) = T
    and is-movable?(puzzle, entity) = T
     ⇒ (pointer-dragging?(pick(puzzle)) = T;
```

is-attached?(pick(puzzle),entity) = T)^3

pointer-within?(puzzle, entity1) = T
   and is-invisible?(puzzle, entity1) = T
     and is-attached?(puzzle,entity) = T
     and
is-acceptable?(puzzle,entity,entity1) =

accepted?((drop(puzzle),entity)) = T;
 is-attached? ((drop(puzzle),entity)) = F;
    // pointer-is-free?
  (drop(puzzle)) = T)

Note: for all other combinations no change in state occurs.

---

[3] The change of state caused by pick is described by changes in two queries, pointer-dragging? and is-attached?. The use of [.] is short for writing the effects on each of the enclosed queries separately.

13
Java and Threaded Containers

Java was developed as an object-oriented language especially suited to programming for the World Wide Web. It can be regarded as a kind of hybrid between C++ and Smalltalk. Syntactically, it resembles the former. Java is more similar to Smalltalk, however, in several semantic respects. It is interpreted rather than compiled into executable form. Its suitability as an open language for Web programming stems from the fact that source code is translated into an intermediate form, called *bytecode*, which can be interpreted on major platforms such as PCs, Macs, and Unix workstations. This enables code residing on a server to be sent to a client for interpretation. This means that users can transparently run applications, called *applets*, that were developed at some other remote site.

13.1 Basic Java

Let's first look at the basic syntax and concepts of Java. Since it looks very much like C++, we can examine the way HCCL is transcribed from C++ to Java as a means to compare and contrast. Here is an extract of the definition of class entity with comments highlighting the similarities and differences.

```
class entity { // Java uses class concepts similar to that of C++

static String classname = "entity";

    // private is the default accessibility mode
    // class variables can be declared and defined at the same time

protected String name; // String is a Java class for strings

protected entity right;

        //pointers are implicit (not explicit as in C++)

public entity( String NAME ){

{name = NAME; right = null;} //null is the official null object

/* entity::~entity(){} */
    // Java does all garbage collection
```

```
                        // so no need for destructors

    public boolean equal(entity ENT)
            // boolean is a Java class with
                    // true and false values
    {
      return
       get_classname().
         compareTo(ENT.get_classname()) == 0
         && get_ent() == ENT ;
            // compareTo is a method of class String
            // the "." notation is used for sending messages
      }
    public entity equal_self(entity ENT)
    {
      if ( equal(ENT) )
       return this;  // self-reference as in C++
      else return null;
    }
    public void print()
    { System.out.println( get_name()); }
    ...
    } // no semi-colon is used to end class definition
```

In contrast to C++, Java supports only single inheritance, which sets up inheritance hierarchies like those described in this book. To see how derived classes are introduced, let's
examine the following example from HCCL.

```
class set extends bag {
    // declares set as derived from class bag
public void add(entity ent)
{
 if (!is_in(ent))
  super.add(ent);
   // use add method of unique parent in class hierarchy.
   // Java doesn't use global method names and only the
   // the superclass methods are invokable by name
}
public set()
{super();}
   // superclass constructors can be invoked like any method
 ...
}
```

Java employs the main function within a class to start execution:

```
class TestEnt { // use class to execute program
public static void main () { // main program
entity e = new container(); // new constructs instances
(container)e.print(); // cast down as in C++
}}
```

13.2 Distinctive Java Features

Java has some features not found in C++. These are some of the main ones:

- abstract classes: provide high-level classes at the top of inheritance hierarchies whose methods would be considered virtual in C++. Such classes cannot have any instances.
- final methods: at the opposite extreme from abstract class methods, such methods are final in the sense that they cannot be overriden when inherited.
- packages: provide a means of encapsulating related classes together so that they can all be imported into a program together. Classes can be hidden within packages so that they are not visible to clients of the package, bringing information hiding to a level above classes. Packages can be organized into hierarchies as well.
- interfaces: can be "mixed in" to provide a restricted means of multiple inheritance. A class can be declared to implement one or more interfaces and thus inherit their declarations. However, these declarations must be only variables or nonimplemented methods, so the class cannot inherit actual code but must supply it itself.
- exception handling: exceptions, such as attempting to remove from an empty container, can be systematically managed so that appropriate notices or corrective actions are initiated.

13.3 Ensemble Methods in Java

Ensemble methods offer a challenge for Java implementation for two reasons:

1. Unlike C++, Java does not have a preprocessor

2. Java does support multithreading.

The first reason means that we do not have the ability to write macros enabling ensemble methods to flexibly accept method names and other arguments. The second reason, however, gives us the ability to implement ensemble methods in a truly parallel/distributed processing environment. Working within these constraints, we'll discuss an approach to implementing ensemble methods in Java.

To understand threads, let's start with a most straightforward example: how to have each entity in a container print out its name by running a thread through each one. Java has a class Thread whose instances can all be executing in parallel on a multiprocessor system or in virtual parallelism in the sense that a single processor will allocate a certain amount of execution time to each one in turn. Each such instance corresponds to the general programming concept of *thread*. We can easily extend class Thread so as to accept an entity argument in its constructor:

```
class printThread extends Thread {
protected entity e;
printThread (entity E) {e = E;}
```

Telling the thread what to do when executed is specified by overriding its run method:

```
public void run(){
e.print();
}}
```

Now, we can arrange to have threads started up with the entities in a container. For example, we could define a method for class container:

```
public void printall
{
for (element p=get_head();p!=null;p = p.get_right())
{
printThread pt = new printThread( p.get_ent());
    pt.start();
}}
```

Here we visit each element in a container and create a new thread for its entity. We start up each such thread using the Thread method start. This is illustrated in Figure 1. Note that we don't wait for one thread to finish before starting another. Thus all threads can be executing in parallel. Of course, for true parallelism, each must be executing on a separate processor and printing on its own screen. Nevertheless, multithreading can still make a big performance difference on a single processor. This happens when you have many jobs to do, such as downloading files and editing files, that differ greatly in their execution-time requirements. If each is being managed by a thread, then the faster jobs such as editing can be done while the slower jobs, in effect, run in the background.

Multithreading is also important for graphical interfaces – many windows and other graphical objects can be active simultaneously.

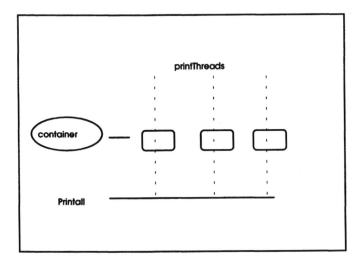

Figure 1. Printing a container's entity names with threads.

13.4 General Approach to Ensemble Methods in Java

Recall that Java does not supply a macro facility that would alleviate the need to rewrite the scanning code in printall each time it is required for a different command or query. The best we can do is provide a framework that saves much labor as possible, and makes clear how to write a desired ensemble method for a particular application. Figure 2 illustrates a class hierarchy that does this. To define an ensemble method for an application, we need to define an appropriate extension of class ensemble and a matching subclass of entityContainerThread.

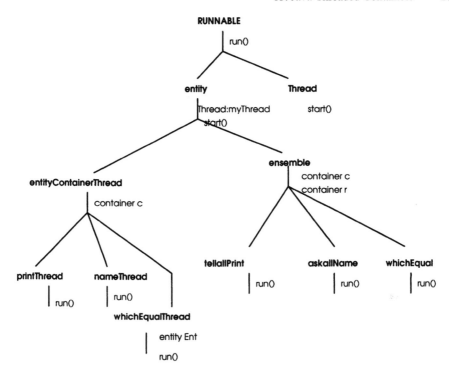

Figure 2. Java class hierarchy to support ensemble method development.

To see how this works, let's start at the top. Runnable is an interface that supports the facilities required by the run method. The instances of any class that implements Runnable can have any number of threads running through its implemented run method. Class Thread also implements Runnable, so it also has a run method. It executes this method unless it is given another Runnable instance explicitly, in which case it executes that instance's run method.

To provide class entity execution capability, we have it implement Runnable and give it a Thread instance variable:

```
class entity implements Thread{
  protected Thread myThread;
entity(){
  myThread = new Thread(this);
  ...
}
```

```
public start(){

myThread.start();

}

...

}
```

Two classes are derived from entity and inherit its execution capability. entityContainerThread provides entity and container instance variables for ensemble method use. The programmer must add additional instance variables to hold incoming arguments; for example, as in the case of whichEqualThread, an entity to holds one argument.

```
class entityContainerThread extends entity {

protected container c;

public entityContainerTThread(entity E){

e = E;

}

public entityContainerThread(entity E,container C){

e = E;

c = C;

}}
```

Likewise, the ensemble subclass of entity supplies two containers, one to be scanned and one for results. Class ensemble must be extended to provide the particular code needed for scanning the first container. Note that since ensemble contains a thread, it can be started at any time within the execution of another thread. This supports application to hierarchical containers.[1]

---

[1] Why not let container itself serve as the base class for all ensemble extensions? Consider tellAllPrint – being derived from container, it cannot be used with any other class. In contrast, the container slot in ensemble can accommodate any derived class of container by polymorphism.

```
class ensemble extends entity{

protected container c;

protected container r;

public ensemble(container C) {

c = C;

r = new container();

}

public container results(){

waitForAllThreads(); 2

return r;

}

}
```

To reimplement printing of container contents, we provide extensions for the entity and ensemble classes:

```
class printThread extends entityContainerThread {

public void run(){

print();

}}
```

---

2 This "barrier" is needed to prevent returning the results container before all threads have finished. Its definition is not difficult but beyond the scope of this book.

```
class tellallPrint extends ensemble{
public tellallPrint(container C){super(C) ;}
public void run() {
for (element p=c.get_head();p != null;p = p.get_right())
    {
  nameThread nt = new nameThread(p.get_ent());
      nt.start();
  }
}}
```

A test of this implementation might look as follows:

```
class TestTellallPrint{
public static void main () {
entity ent1 = new entity ("ent1");
entity ent2 = new entity ("ent2");
container c = new container();
c.add(ent1);
c.add(ent2);
tellallPrint tc = new tellallPrint(c);
tc.start();
}}
```

Notice that we can make full use of polymorphism – any subclass of container can be input to tellallPrint, and the container can have any subtype of entity as its contents. To enable printing of a hierarchical container, we create a tellallPrint instance within the print method of container:

```
public void print{
tellallPrint tc = new tellallPrint(this);
tc.start();
}
```

The normal polymorphism rules apply when the entity in a container happens to be a container itself (recall the discussion of hierarchical methods in the Problems of Chapter 6). In this case, the print method will be executed, which in turn starts up a new Thread to print the container.

Implementing Askall and Which?

Implementing an askall method can build upon the experience with tellall. We define extensions for classes ensemble and entityContainerThread:

```
class askallName extends ensemble{
public askallName (container C) {super(C);}
public void run(){
{ for (element p=c.get_head();p!=null;p= p.get_right()) {
  nameThread nt = new nameThread(p.get_ent(),r);
    nt.start();
}}
```

```
class nameThread extends entityContainerThread {
public void run(){
c.add(new entity(get_name()));
}}
```

As before, we can package askallName as a method of container:

```
public get_names(){
askallName t = new askallName(this);
t.start();
 return t.results();
}
```

13.5 Synchronization

There is, however, a complication that arises in askallName, which is illustrated in Figure 3. Notice that the threads for the entities in the source container may be concurrently attempting to add items to the results container. Unless we take preventive action, a thread can be suspended in the middle of processing its add method, in favor of another thread that can start its own add method processing. This can wreak havoc since each thread can leave the container in an inconsistent state with respect to the other.

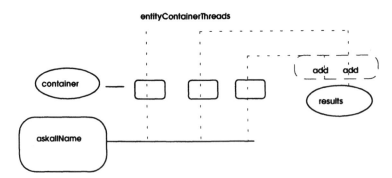

Figure 3. Illustrating the need for Synchronization.

To ensure that threads mutually exclude themselves in critical methods, Java provides *synchronization* features. For example, the add method of container can be made *thread-safe* by adding the synchronizing specification:

```
public synchronized void add (entity E){

    ...

}
```

Now Threads must wait for the current Thread to complete its processing of the add method. Only one Thread can be performing such processing at a time. Of course, this is now a potential bottleneck to slow down processing.[3] So we'll want to keep the use of such synchronization to a minimum.

---

[3] The extent to which such "barrier" synchronization is a bottleneck depends on how fast threads accumulate there relative to how fast they are "serviced". In the ideal case, the time required for each thread to compute its entity's response is much larger than the time required to add the response to the target container. In this case, most of the work is done in parallel.

Adding Capability to Transmit Arguments

So far the queries and commands multicast by the ensemble methods have not required arguments. To add this capability, we can extend entity ContainerThread to include placeholders for such arguments. For example, to implement a which? ensemble method such as whichEqual (which entities in a container are equal to a given entity?), we can do the following:

```
class whichEqual extends ensemble{
protected entity Ent;
public whichEqual(container C,entity E) {
super(C);
Ent = E;
}
public void run(){
{
for
(element p=c.get_head();p!=null;p= p.get_right()) {
whichEqualThread nt = new whichEqualThread( p.get_ent(), Ent,r);
    nt.start();
}
```

Here the extension of entityContainerThread is defined with an additional instance variable, Ent. This enables it to store the argument passed by whichEqual for use in the execution of the run method. The implementation is given by

```
class whichEqualThread extends entityContainerThread {
public entity Ent;
public whichEqualThread(entity E, entity ENT, container C){
super(E,C);
Ent = ENT;
}
public void run(){
if (e.equal(Ent)) c.add(e);
}}
```

13.6 Hierarchical Graphics Construction in Java

Java provides support for hierarchical construction of *graphical user interfaces* (GUIs) through its abstract window tool kit. In the class hierarchy that forms this tool kit, the Container class can contain graphical objects, called Components. As illustrated in Figure 4, class Components includes buttons, scrollbars, drawing canvasses, and other commonly employed interface objects. Since Container is also an extension of Component (just as container extends entity in HCCL), hierarchical construction is enabled. Such construction greatly simplifies the task of building complex interfaces. For example, Figure 5 illustrates a GUI that consists of a TextField and two identical Panels. A Panel is composed of a Canvas, a Scrollbar, and two Buttons with specific dimensions and placed in specific locations. Hierarchical construction allows us to layout the Panel once and then make any number of copies of it. In contrast, if Components could not be used to make larger Components, then each low-level component (buttons, canvasses, and so on) would have to be individually configured and located on the overall Panel – a very tedious and errorprone task.

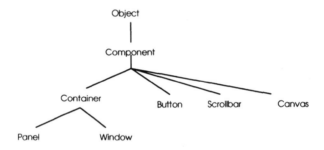

Figure 4. Java class hierarchy (partial).

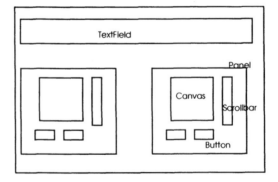

Figure 5. Example of a Java GUI.

13.6 Summary

This book comes to an end in full circle with its beginning. We began with the premise that it is valuable to be able to specify object behavior before implementing it. One of the important reasons is that a specification can have a longer lifetime than any of its implementations – indeed, it may be implemented to take advantage of emerging technologies. In this chapter, we have seen how the specification of the Container class hierarchy remained invariant as we migrated the implementation from C++ to Java. The multithreading capabilities of Java enabled us to implement the ensemble methods so as to exploit their intrinsic parallelism and speed up their execution. One certainty about the future is that technologies will continue to evolve. The ability to work with abstract concepts – which are much more stable than their concrete realizations – will enable software developers to stay ahead of the ever-evolving technology development curve.

Problems

1. Implement the remaining ensemble methods (which-one? and reduce) in Java using multithreading. Test your implementations using a test suite that is predesigned and based on their specified behavior.

2. Some ensemble methods, such as which-one?, some?, and all?, can, under certain conditions, have their execution terminated as soon as an answer is definitely known. Write implementations that kill all outstanding threads once a known-to-be-final answer is obtained. (*Hint:* send the Thread method stop() to a Container of threads that have not yet completed.)

3. The execution order of threads in Java is controlled by a scheduler. The operation can be emulated as follows: class scheduler is derived from class order. When a thread is created, it is added to a scheduler instance with a given priority. The threads currently in the scheduler are ordered by priority; those having the same priority are ordered according to time spent waiting since last receiving execution. The thread chosen for next execution is the one highest in priority with the most time spent waiting since last receiving execution. This thread is given some execution and then returned to schedule unless it has completed its execution. Implement your own classes thread and schedule to model the thread management algorithm just discussed.

4. Write an object behavior specification for a button that toggles between the on and off states each time it is pressed. (*Hint:* compare with the binary counter in Chapter 1.) Contrast this toggle switch behavior with a pair of check boxes (checking one box unchecks the other).)

5. Implement the face puzzle specified in Chapter 12. Use Java's abstract window class hierarchy to realize the graphical objects as well as the multithreaded implementations of ensemble methods given in this chapter.

6. Implement a simulation of the house alarm system discussed in Chapter 12. Provide a GUI that depicts the layout of the house and the alarm placement. Animate the flashing/sounding of alarms and the actions of door opening/closings in a break-in.

Index

Printed in Great Britain
by Amazon